DEMYTHOLOGIZING
CELIBACY

Practical Wisdom
from Christian and Buddhist Monasticism

William Skudlarek, OSB

LITURGICAL PRESS
Collegeville, Minnesota

www.litpress.org

Cover design by David Manahan, OSB. Photo by Lee Hanley.

1   2   3   4   5   6   7   8   9

Library of Congress Cataloging-in-Publication Data

Skudlarek, William.
    Demythologizing celibacy : practical wisdom from Christian and Buddhist monasticism / William Skudlarek.
        p. cm.
    Includes bibliographical references.
    ISBN 978-0-8146-2947-5
    1. Celibacy—Catholic Church—Comparative studies.
2. Monastic and religious life—Comparative studies.
3. Celibacy—Buddhism—Comparative studies.   4. Monastic and religious life (Buddhism)—Comparative studies.   I. Title.

BX2435.S555 2008
248.4'7—dc22   2007046544

Contents

Introduction

In the early seventies one of America's most well-known and well-published Catholic writers came out with a book called *The Jesus Myth*.[1] The author was Father Andrew Greeley, and many Christians were understandably shocked when they saw the title, assuming he intended to call into question the Christian faith in Jesus as the incarnate Son of God. Upon reading the book, however, they quickly discovered—as Greeley made clear in a prefatory note—that he was using the word "myth" to mean not legend, but a symbolic story that reveals the inner meaning of the universe and human life.[2]

Celibacy has become a myth, but in two quite different senses. As a result of the recent and intense media coverage of clergy sexual abuse, many now believe that celibacy is a myth in the commonly accepted sense of the term and regard it as pure fiction, little more than a hypocritical cover-up for widespread promiscuity and abusive behavior.

At the same time, a long Catholic tradition of speaking about celibacy as a higher calling, a special charism given to a few privileged souls, has transformed celibacy into a myth by presenting it as a quasi-angelic way of life, beyond the reach of ordinary mortals. This mythologized notion of celibacy would frequently be spoken of in language so rarified that it rarely if ever dealt with the actual practice or experience of this particular way of life.

This double mythologizing of celibacy—dismissing it on the one hand, divinizing it on the other—has made it almost impossible to think or speak of it as a normal—though admittedly not common—way of life, one that is especially suited to those who are intent on devoting themselves to developing the life of the spirit.

Conversation with Buddhist monks who maintain their ancient tradition of following the celibate path is one way of coming to understand that celibacy can be lived with integrity and can be meaningful without being in any way connected to the "myth" of Jesus or even belief in a personal God.

The seeds for this book were sown in October 2004 when fourteen Buddhist and Catholic monks who reside in North America came together for the first meeting of "Monks in the West." The conference was organized by Monastic Interreligious Dialogue (MID), the North American branch of an international organization of Catholic monks and nuns committed to fostering interreligious and intermonastic dialogue at the level of spiritual practice and experience. The meeting was hosted by Dharma Master Heng Lyu and Reverend Heng Sure at the City of Ten Thousand Buddhas in Ukiah, California. Representatives of various monastic traditions within Buddhism and Catholicism spent two full days together sharing their experience of the rewards and challenges of living the monastic life in a Western secular culture. I was privileged to be part of that conversation.

We devoted the first day of our meeting to spiritual autobiographies. Each of us recounted what drew us to the monastic way of life and, more important, what keeps us there. Some of the participants said they knew they wanted to be a monk when they were still young boys; for others the attraction to monastic life came later in life, after they had undergone an existential crisis ("I am going to die") or experienced the emptiness and sometimes bitter aftertaste of material success and sensual pleasure.

For some, becoming a monk meant going to a far-off land to embrace a new and exotic culture; for others being in the monastery was not all that different from the life they had experienced growing up in a tightly knit ethnic or religious community where everyone shared the same values and customs. In some cases the monastic life offered expanded opportunities for education, work, and travel; for others it demanded they renounce the success they had achieved and the possibility of further advancement in a chosen profession.

Some who became celibate monks had been married or in one or more relationships; others acknowledged that they entered monastic life without ever having experienced a sexual relationship, or even because they were afraid of their sexuality and wanted to avoid dealing with it. More often than not, they discovered that denial and repression only made it more difficult to deal with sexual issues later in life.

There were stories of difficult relationships with superiors or confreres, some of which continued to cause pain and distrust. Others spoke of superiors who trusted and supported them during times of vocational crisis and in this way helped them to trust themselves and to deepen their commitment to the way of life they had chosen.

Stories were told of the struggle to remain faithful to contemplative monastic practices while responding to the many demands that are made of monks—especially of superiors—either by their own communities or by others. "How can we keep our best monks from burning out?" was a question that was asked repeatedly.

Toward the end of the meeting, as we named some of the common questions and concerns that emerged, we acknowledged how often we had expressed our conviction that monastic life, lived fully and well, is a powerful expression of a rich and fully human existence. Since both Buddhist and Catholic monks refrain from sexual activity and from the possession of personal property, we asked what it is about these central monastic renunciations that help a monk become a well-rounded, authentic human being.

When we turned to the question of holding a future meeting, the rapport, friendship, and encouragement we had experienced left little doubt that we wanted to continue our relationship. We also wanted to invite other monks to experience the richness of an interreligious conference that focused specifically on monastic issues.

The topic for a follow-up meeting emerged quickly and was unanimously accepted: "Authentic Practices of Celibacy and Intimacy in Monastic Communities of Men." We agreed to meet again in two years to examine the teaching of our respective monastic traditions on celibacy as well as to consider how celibacy is actually lived out in our monastic communities. Our purpose in doing this would be to learn from one another how we might live the monastic life more authentically and thereby become more fully integrated and self-transcending human beings.

Monks in the West II took place at Saint John's Abbey in Collegeville, Minnesota, in October 2006. Twelve Buddhists joined ten Catholics for a three-day conversation on celibacy and the monastic way of life. The conference was divided into three parts: the "Why" of celibacy (*Theoria*); the "How" of celibacy (*Praxis*); the "What if . . ." of celibacy (*Therapia*).

Each discussion was introduced by presentations on Buddhist and Catholic approaches to the topic, one of which, Brother Gregory Perron's paper, "Entering the Heart of our Heart: A Reflection on the Why of Catholic Monastic Celibacy," appears in full in Monastic Interreligious Dialogue's online Bulletin (no. 78): www.monasticdialogue.org/.

This book is not intended to be a report on Monks in the West II per se.[3] Rather, it might best be described as a modest effort to demythologize, reevaluate, and reflect on the meaning and practice of Catholic celibacy—specifically Catholic *monastic* celibacy—in the light of some Buddhist teachings and practices as these were heard and understood by a Catholic participant. If certain aspects of the tradition and practice of celibacy are treated in detail while other important dimensions are only alluded to, the reason—in part, at least—is that my reflections on celibacy were shaped by the presentations that were given prior to each session of the conference: Venerable Kusala Bhikshu and Brother Gregory Perron, OSB, on *Theoria*; Venerable Berthold Olson and Father Terrence Kardong, OSB, on *Praxis*; Ajahn Punnadhammo and Abbot John Klassen, OSB, on *Therapia*. Since the entire conference was recorded, it was possible to incorporate insights and points of view that emerged during the course of

the discussions. I also used and wish to acknowledge with gratitude a paper Reverend Jisho Perry wrote in preparation for the
conference in which he developed a Buddhist understanding of
the meaning and purpose of monastic celibacy.

Along with the other Catholic monks who took part in the
conference, I was deeply impressed by our Buddhist brothers'
commitment to the practice of celibacy as a path to liberation
and wisdom, as well as by their understanding and willing acceptance of the demands of a chaste celibate life. As we listened
to one another, we became more conscious of significant differences between some Buddhist teachings and practices and those
of the Christian tradition. However, rather than concluding that
if one view is accepted as right, the other must be rejected as
wrong, we recognized that the teachings and practices of different spiritual traditions can complement one another, and that a
particular spiritual path can only be fully understood and ap-
preciated by those who have chosen to walk it.

When people of diverse religious traditions speak openly of
their personal convictions and listen nonjudgmentally to the convictions of others, they often become more appreciative of the
strengths of their own beliefs and practices, and, at the same time,
more aware of their weaknesses. That was certainly true for the
Catholic monks who participated in Monks in the West II. As we
grew in our understanding of celibacy as a path to spiritual growth,
we recognized the ways in which the Christian teaching and practice of celibacy have been shaped by and given expression to a
deep love for God and neighbor. But we also recognized that the
Christian understanding and practice of celibacy have been distorted by misogyny and an exaggerated suspicion of the body.

Another important awareness that emerged from this conference was how uncritically Catholics tend to think and speak
about the monastic way of life (and therefore about celibacy) as
a uniquely Christian phenomenon. Nothing could be further
from the truth. To "demythologize" celibacy also means becoming aware that at its deepest level monasticism is an expression
of something fundamental to the human person: the thirst for
that which is ultimate. For that reason, some have spoken of a

monastic "archetype" present in every human being.[4] The monk is one who willingly—though not always without pain—renounces lesser goods, choosing "blessed simplicity" in order to devote himself entirely to the pursuit of what will fully satisfy his longing.

Celibacy is further "demythologized" when we become conscious of the fact that monasticism as an institutionalized, celibate way of life in support of an intense search for meaning, integration, and perfection flourished in the Hindu and Buddhist world of Southeast and East Asia centuries before the birth of Jesus and continues to be practiced by contemporary monks of these religious traditions. Christian monasticism articulates the archetypal monastic vocation by making it into a response to Jesus' invitation to seek perfection by abandoning everything, caring for the poor, and following him: "If you wish to be perfect, go, sell your possessions, and give the money to the poor, and you will have treasure in heaven; then come, follow me. . . . And everyone who has left houses[5] or brothers or sisters or father or mother or children or fields, for my name's sake, will receive a hundredfold, and will inherit eternal life" (Matt 19:21, 29). By adding this specifically Christian understanding to the practice of celibacy—itself a "natural" rather than "supernatural" phenomenon—Christian monks demonstrate the meaning of the dictum of Scholastic theology that grace supposes and builds on nature (*gratia supponit naturam*); it does not supplant or destroy it.

Celibacy is the most characteristic feature of the monk, male or female. In his masterful work on John Cassian my confrere, Father Columba Stewart, speaks of the intentional celibacy of the monastic life as "the principal marker of its social distinctiveness."[6] Its meaning and significance for Christian monks will be closely related to their desire to follow Jesus by giving their lives to God alone. But celibacy also has enormous meaning and significance for monks who are not Christians or theists. Once we come to know and appreciate the spiritual witness of monks from other religious traditions, it is no longer possible to say that celibacy can only be lived with integrity and generosity if it is understood as an expression of total and exclusive devotion to

Christ, to the kingdom of God, and to the church. This is the meaning celibacy has for Christians, but to imply that it is the only reason for celibacy fails to take into account the wisdom to be found in the teaching and practice of a monastic tradition that predates ours by at least six centuries and continues to enrich the world today.

I should be clear at the outset that this book will not address the important and thorny question of obligatory celibacy for Roman Catholic priests. The focus here is on chaste celibacy as an essential component—along with the renunciation of personal property and egoism—of the monastic or, more generally, the vowed religious life. Nor does it address the question of celibacy for women, and thus gender specific language will generally be used.

Finally, it should be noted that while the teaching of the Trappist monk, Thomas Merton, was very much a part of Monks in the West II, especially in the presentation and discussion on the "why" of celibacy from the Catholic point of view, Merton's personal struggles with celibacy toward the end of his life were never alluded to, much less discussed. Nonetheless, I have decided to devote an entire chapter to this crucial period of Merton's life because it so clearly and dramatically demonstrates the meaning of celibacy for those called to the monastic life and the struggle of one monk to remain true to his calling.

Monks in the West II was made possible, in part, by a generous grant to Monastic Interreligious Dialogue from the Council of Men and Women Presidents of the American Benedictine Congregations and Federations. MID is most grateful to the council for its support of interreligious dialogue that takes place at the level of spiritual experience and practice. I also wish to express my deep appreciation to the Reverend Heng Sure and to Mr. Lee Hanley for their encouragement and helpful suggestions.

William Skudlarek, OSB
June 24, 2007
Feast of the Nativity of Saint John the Baptist
Patron of Monks

Chapter 1

One Path,
Different Destinations

Buddhist and Catholic Motives for Celibacy

One of the constant refrains in more popular writings and conversations on the subject of interreligious dialogue is that we are all on different religious paths, but heading toward the same goal. Regarding celibacy, however, and monastic celibacy in particular, it seems truer to say that Catholics and Buddhists follow the same path, but the path takes them to different destinations.

Catholic monks choose to forego marriage and to seek solitude—most often in company with other seekers—in order to love God with their whole heart, and mind and soul and to love their neighbor as themselves (see Matt 22:34-40). The essential solitude of the monastic life is more clearly evident in those Catholic monastic orders that emphasize the eremitic form of monasticism, for example the Carthusians or the Camaldolese. But solitude is also a value for cenobites—monks who live in community—because a monastic community is not simply a gathering of like-minded individuals who enjoy one another's company and work together on a common project. It is, rather, an intentional community whose members are dedicated to the work of spiritual growth and who together fashion an environment in which each can engage in that inner work with a minimum of distractions.[1]

In addition to being a *schola caritatis*, a laboratory for testing and strengthening the day-to-day practice of unselfish fraternal love, a monastic community exists to create an environment in

1

which solitude is cherished and protected. Although many are drawn to the monastic life in the hope of finding there the ideal community that will meet their needs for companionship and affirmation, it usually does not take long before they begin to chafe under the limits and challenges of life in community. If they are to persevere, they will have to grow in their appreciation for the communal life as an environment that encourages and safeguards the solitude that is essential to self-knowledge and to the knowledge of God as unconditional and self-emptying love.

For Buddhists, on the other hand, celibacy has meaning as a path to wisdom and liberation. A Buddhist monk would not identify love as his motive for choosing to be celibate. Not that the Buddhist sees anything wrong with love. But the idea that love is what is drawing him and waiting for him would confuse him—and yet attract him at the same time.

The path of celibacy is the same for both Buddhist and Christian monks, but the goal for the Buddhist is liberation from *dukkha*, a word often translated as suffering but better understood as the ultimately unsatisfying character of human existence. To say that love is the goal of celibacy would not provide a sufficient rationale for the Buddhist, for whom liberation is the ultimate goal of human existence.

And yet within Buddhism there are nuances. Although the goal of the Buddhist is personal liberation (*nirvana*) where dukkha comes to an end, there is also the ideal of the Bodhisattva, the compassionate one who puts off nirvana in order to seek the end of dukkha for all living beings. Still, for a Buddhist there are questions that remain: Is love the highest good, or is there something beyond love, beyond compassion? Once one has arrived at completely selfless love, what is that experience like? Is there still a self that can love selflessly? Or has the self been dissolved?

The Buddhist insistence on liberation as the meaning and purpose of celibacy becomes clearer when we recall the Buddha's teaching on the meaning and goal of human existence.

The essence of the Buddha's insight into the human situation is expressed in the "Four Noble Truths" and the "Noble Eightfold Path":

1. Life is ultimately (though not always) unsatisfying. Everyone who is born will get sick, grow old, and die. Everything that makes us happy will be taken away. Nothing lasts forever, and there is nothing we can do about it.
2. Desire is what makes life so unsatisfying. We are selfish; we have a thirst, a craving that cannot ever be satisfied. We either want more, or we become attached to what we have, wanting it to last forever. We know it cannot, and that knowledge distresses us.
3. There is an end to dukkha, an end to this seemingly endless experience of the misery of life. It is possible to exist without being reborn into the same experience of dissatisfaction, and that way of existing is nirvana.
4. There is a way to nirvana: the Noble Eightfold Path
   a) Right view
   b) Right intention
   c) Right speech
   d) Right action
   e) Right livelihood
   f) Right effort
   g) Right mindfulness
   h) Right concentration

The key insight of the Buddha in relation to sexuality and celibacy lies in identifying sexual pleasure as the most powerful sensual pleasure, the one to which we become most easily and strongly attached. To attain the highest way of life, it is necessary to relinquish the desire for sexual pleasure because this form of gratification obstructs the concentration (*samadhi*), the one-pointed stillness that leads to insight (wisdom). If some sensory data are more desirable, they become harder to let go of, and the mind will return to duality.

Refraining from sexual misconduct is the third of the basic training rules for Buddhist practitioners, known as the "five precepts," that is, the five lay precepts (*panca sila*):

1. to refrain from destroying living creatures;
2. to refrain from taking that which is not given;

3. to refrain from sexual misconduct;
4. to refrain from incorrect speech;
5. to refrain from intoxicating drinks and drugs, which lead to carelessness.

One commentator points out that in the third of these precepts for householders (i.e., laypersons), the word *kama* refers to any form of sensual pleasure, but with an emphasis on sexual pleasure. A literal translation of the precept would be "I take the rule of training (*veramani sikkhapadam samadiyami*) not to go the wrong way (*micchacara*) for sexual pleasure (*kamesu*). Thus, the Buddha is not prohibiting sexual pleasure as such, but only "misconduct for sexual pleasure."[2]

The monastic application of this training rule goes one step further: Giving up all attachment to sensual pleasure, of which the sexual is the most intense and leads to strongest attachment, is regarded as fundamental to one who has dedicated his life to spiritual development. In the teaching of the Buddha, sensual pleasures simply do not and cannot deliver the ultimate happiness we are looking for. On the contrary, they inevitably lead to dukkha.

The Buddha's teaching on the false promises of sensual pleasure is colorfully expressed in a number of similes. Sense pleasure is like bare bones thrown to a dog that do not satisfy its hunger; like a lump of flesh over which birds of prey fight and even kill one another; like a dream of a beautiful landscape that evaporates when one awakes; like borrowed goods over which the borrower prides himself and then is shamed when they are taken back; and so forth. In these similes the Buddha highlighted the deceptive and yet powerful attraction of sensual pleasure and identified it as a significant hindrance for anyone dedicated to finding the way to freedom and complete happiness.

Buddhists regard sexual pleasure as such a devious trap because for many people—perhaps most—the sensual experience that comes closest to spiritual transcendence and offers a foretaste of complete happiness is orgasm. There is indeed a sense of release brought about by the intense physical and emotional pleasure that comes from being aroused sexually. This experience is easily confused with the release from attachment to self that is encouraged by spiritual traditions.

Western secular psychiatric and psychological literature tends to present the quest for spirituality and spiritual experiences as a sublimation of sex. From the Buddhist point of view, it may be just the other way around: orgasm may actually be an ersatz experience of transcendence. If that is true, the reason for celibacy is that it allows one to go for the real goods, for true self-transcendence. One is not shortchanged by an experience that only gives a glimpse, at best, of transcendence. One does not, as T. S. Elliot put it in *Four Quartets*, have the experience, but miss the meaning.[3]

The Buddhist case for celibacy is also related to an Eastern understanding of the flow of bodily energies. The movement of the body's energy in meditation flows up the spine and over the head and can be likened to a spiritual generator. The movement of this energy is invigorating and leads to deeper spiritual awakening. Channeling this same energy into sexual activity, however, takes the energy down and out, leaving one feeling spent and feeding the delusion that one must continue to pursue this pleasure in order to find happiness.

The effect of the sexual act on the human mind is not unlike the way certain drugs create a condition of dependency. Just as an alcoholic or a drug addict cannot imagine how life could be bearable without alcohol or drugs, so those who find pleasure in sex cannot conceive of the possibility of enjoying life without it. However, if one is to grow in the spiritual life and to experience liberation from dissatisfaction, one must be able to let go of attachments, especially, some might say, one's attachment to the pleasure aroused by sexual activity.

Buddhist monks refrain from sexual activity not because it is intrinsically bad or immoral, but because it inevitably results in attachment and, consequently, dukkha. Without an end to sexual activity there is no end to dukkha. Buddhist training, especially monastic training, places great emphasis on relinquishing one's attachment to desire, recognizing how well-nigh impossible it is to give up desire while actively pursing sexual gratification.

A crucial element of relinquishing attachment to desire is not "entertaining" lustfulness. The fact that lustful desires arise is not the problem; that happens naturally. What is problematic is nurturing and entertaining these desires. Doing so only creates more attachment. On the other hand, simply noting lustful thoughts and desires as they arise and then allowing them to depart without acting on them is another step toward freedom.

According to Dogen Zenji, the thirteenth-century Japanese Buddhist who brought the Zen meditation tradition from China and founded the Soto branch of Zen Buddhism, spiritual adequacy is found in letting go of desire. If one knows one's true adequacy there is nothing more to be desired. Indeed, all human desires can be seen as an expression of the one desire to know True Peace, the fundamental tranquility of the Buddha Nature.

One Buddhist way of describing True Peace would be to say it consists in living a normal life in the world, wanting nothing, having nothing, and knowing nothing, being serene in all trouble and compassionate to all life. To live in this way is to experience true happiness. To live in this way is to be a Buddha.

In Buddhism this "nothing" has many meanings and is expressed in a multitude of ways. It is, however, not a negative void, but rather an expression of what can be called "Emptiness," "Ultimate Truth," "Mu," "Buddha Nature," "The Unborn," "The Lord of the House," or "The Deathless." Reverend Master Jiyu-Kennett, founder of the Order of Buddhist Contemplatives and first abbess of Shasta Abbey, referred to this "nothing" as the "Fullest Emptiness you will ever know." It can be experienced as the giving up of desire, knowing the Truth, casting off of body and mind, dissolving into the universe, and the giving up of the self. These and other expressions are very similar to those found in the mystical traditions of all religions.

The spiritual aspiration of a Buddhist is to work for the good of all living things. A particularly powerful and exalted expression of this aspiration is the monastic commitment to renounce worldly goods and behaviors. Celibacy is regarded as a su-

premely beneficial, if not essential, dimension of this renunciation. If celibacy were to be seen as a repression of sexuality, it
would be harmful. Without accepting desire as a natural part of
the human condition, one cannot transcend it.

Having experienced a sexual relationship is not a hindrance
to arrive eventually at a complete understanding of the truth, as
the life of the Buddha demonstrates. He was married and had a
child before renouncing the world and becoming a monk. Attachment to desire, however, is a hindrance to spiritual progress.
The wholehearted commitment required of the monastic life
requires the relinquishment of all distractions, all attachments,
that create a barrier or hindrance to spiritual development.

Celibacy is a powerful force that allows one to see through
the delusion of desire and know true peace. Celibacy allows the
energy of the body and mind to be used in harmony in order to
go deeper into spiritual understanding and to know both Great
Compassion and Great Wisdom. The difficulties and conflicts
created by and with self-restraint are clarified by spiritual insight and understanding that come as a result of the training.
One has to be able to find a true refuge in spiritual practice in
order to do this. It is necessary to discover that one is more at
peace by not engaging in sexual relations than by doing so.

The cultural delusion being sold by a secularized Western
culture is that sexual activity is necessary, pleasurable, essential
to good health, and without any harmful consequences. The
experience of countless numbers of individuals, however, indi-
cates that this is not necessarily true. There are celibates who
have become mature, healthy individuals, while some who engaged freely in sexual activity have become profoundly disil-
lusioned and bitter. A celibate monk who is at peace is able to
look at others without focusing on gender, attractiveness, likes,
dislikes, expectations, jealousy, hurt feelings and all the other
emotional consequences of attachments that so frequently follow from sexual contact. By not looking at others through the
filter of desire, one can see everyone as a Buddha.

Sexual activity with another person involves the most intense and powerful form of human contact, a contact that is

central to the grasping that creates attachment and is the source of dukkha. Buddhist teachings are focused on seeing how dukkha is created and how it is cured. Letting go of the things that have, in the past, created attachments and dukkha is essential to successful Buddhist practice. Celibacy plays an important part in the conversion of our ignorance regarding desire. Renouncing sex as bad or harmful is not helpful; what is important is knowing that there is something far better than the pleasure brought about by sexual activity and then taking the necessary steps to arrive there.

For Christian monks, celibacy is ultimately about love.

The Christian understanding of God and our relationship to God is most perfectly summed up in the words of the apostle John, who says that God is love, and that those who abide in love abide in God, and God in them (1 John 4:16). To be the image of God (see Gen 1:26) means to be endowed with the capacity to love God and neighbor as God loves us, that is, not for our sake, but for the sake of the other. A Christian is not someone who has an exclusive claim on this love of God for us or on our capacity for selfless love. Rather, a Christian is one who believes and affirms that in Jesus Christ God's love became flesh and lives among us (John 1:14), that we are "in Christ,"[4] that our love for God and others is nothing less than the "one Christ loving himself."[5]

All people are called to mirror in their lives the love of God for the world. For most Christians, as for most people in general, the vocation to love is given expression in and through marriage and family. But there will also be those who discover within themselves a mystifying attraction to celibacy—mystifying because it is so out of step with what virtually everyone else regards as "normal," mystifying too because one can be drawn to celibacy and still experience a loving, even sexual, attraction to others.

For some the appeal of celibacy may be closely related to a desire to preserve their independence and freedom so that they can more easily pursue their own interests. But there are those who sense that celibacy is the "skillful means" (to use a helpful

Buddhist expression) by which they will be able to love others without the self-interest and attachment that are an inevitable component of a genital sexual relationship.

There are also individuals who find themselves attracted to celibacy because they know that radical, existential solitude is the very heart of their true self, even though they may not be able to articulate this awareness clearly. Reflecting on his attraction to the eremitic life, the Trappist monk Matthew Kelty says,

> Not that I do not enjoy people. I do. But when I forego company I become something else, or am aware of something more. In fact, I feel I get closer to them and to basic truth that way. So I conclude that this is what I am supposed to do, or perhaps, all that I can do. Trouble is, I guess, that what goes on within is more real to me than what goes on without. And I can only relate to it in a context of solitude. I assume that characterizes a call to this sort of life. But I do not spend time explaining it to myself or others. I am tired of that. Anyway it seems without point. As is usually the case with me, I do something first and then try to find out why afterwards![6]

Without fully understanding their innate desire to withdraw from most forms of normal interaction with other people, some individuals sense that their deep yearning to be loved unconditionally and to love with their whole being will only be realized if they remain *solus cum Solo*, alone with the Only One. Christians who sense that solitude is the way for them to nurture a personal and intimate relationship with God will often feel drawn to the monastic way of life in order to devote themselves entirely to this single-minded search for God.

It may seem strange that the appeal of solitude is what would lead one to the cenobitic life, that is, to a communal rather than an eremitic form of monasticism. However, monasteries are meant to be places where silence and solitude are honored and protected.[7] One can certainly live a life of solitude outside a monastery, but most people are not strong enough for that, either physically or psychologically. They need a rule, an abbot, and the "help of many brethren"[8] in order to remain faithful to the continuing quest for God that is the raison d'être of monastic life for Christians.

The monk, then, is one who understands the need for and treasures solitude, even while daily demonstrating through word and deed his love for his fellow monks. The centrality of solitude in monastic life is to be found in the very word "monk," commonly derived from the Latin *monachus,* a transliteration of the Greek *monachos.* The Greek word, in turn, is generally derived from *monos* meaning "alone."[9] However, it should be noted that early Christian authors who wrote about monasticism had differing opinions about the etymological significance of *monachos/monachus.*

For example, Saint Jerome asks Heliodorus, "Consider the meaning of the word 'monk.' It is, after all, the name you go by. Since you are a solitary, what are you doing in the crowd?"[10] To be a monk, in other words, means quite literally to keep apart from other people, to cease from being "one of the crowd."

Saint Augustine, on the other hand, emphasizes that living in unity with one's brothers is what makes one a monk. In his exposition of Psalm 132 [133] he says,

> Why, then should we not call ourselves monks, since the Psalm says, "Behold how good and how pleasant it is, that brethren should dwell together in one"? *Monos means* "one," but not "one" in any which way. A man in a crowd is one in the sense that he is one of many. He can be called "one," but he cannot be called *monos,* that is, "alone," for μόνος means "one alone." Therefore those who live in unity in such a way as to form one person, so that what has been written can truly be said of them, namely, that they are one mind and one heart—many bodies, but not many minds; many bodies, but not many hearts—can rightly be called *monos,* that is, "one alone."[11]

The Ecclesiastical Hierarchy, the work of a fifth-century Greek writer who tried to pass himself off as the Areopagite converted by St. Paul (see Acts 17:34), says that of all the orders of the initiated, the highest is the holy order of the monks. He notes that some call them "devotees" (*therapeutē*).[12] This may be a reference to the life and customs of the Therapeutae, vegetarian and probably celibate ascetics who appeared in Alexandria shortly before the Christian era and were referred to by Philo, a first-century Hellenized Jewish philosopher from Alexandria, in his work *De vita contemplativa*. It is not a common term. In early Christian literature, the only other place it is found is in the writings of Clement of Alexandria, who died around the year 215.

The reason those who belong to the highest order of the initiated are called "monks," says Dionysius, is "because of their pure service and cult of God as well as on account of their undivided and united life, which unifies them by holy combinations of their differences into godlike unity and perfection of divine love."[13] For Dionysius, what characterizes a monk above all is not that he lives alone (*monos*), apart from the crowd, as Jerome would have it, nor that he lives in unity with his brothers (*monos* in the sense of "*in unum*," "together," "as one"), as Augustine would argue, but that he has realized a purely internal unity (*monas* rather than *monos*), that is, singleness of heart and unity with the One. Thomas Merton reflected this understanding of monastic solitude when he wrote, "The true unity of the solitary life is the one in which there is no possible division. The true solitary does not seek himself, but loses himself. He forgets that there is number, in order to become all."[14]

The explanation of Dionysius is also favored by Anselm Grün, who gives it a Jungian interpretation: "[Dionysius] expressed a profound human longing to overcome the polarity of man and woman, the longing for a human being incorporating within himself both man and woman at the same time; the longing for the androgynous human being who unites in himself masculine and feminine elements."[15]

Dionysius goes on to say, "many things which are done by the middle order [the equivalent of "householders" in Buddhist terminology] without reproach are in every way forbidden to the unified monks, since they ought to unite themselves to the One [and] be gathered into a sacred unit."[16] Among these "many things" Dionysius would include military service, commerce, and marriage.

For monks, celibacy, like intentional simplicity of life, is a tool, a skillful means by which their heart is burrowed out and the core of their being laid bare. By embracing celibacy, monks accept the aloneness that is ultimately the condition of every human being and strive to realize the inner unity that is jeopardized by attachment to sensual pleasure, material possessions, and ego.

Men and women who are profoundly aware that God alone can satisfy their deepest longing to love and be loved do not really choose to be celibate. Rather, they find that they are simply unable to be married, that celibacy has chosen them. They recognize that they are, if not physically, then emotionally and psychologically, "eunuchs from birth" (Matt 19:12). The only way they can give authentic expression to their true identity as lovers is by a conscious decision not to bind themselves to one other person so that they may become one with God, one with everyone. In Merton's words, "He who is alone and is conscious of what his solitude means, finds himself simply in the ground of life. He is 'in Love.' He is in love with all, with everyone, with everything."[17]

The dimension of the Christian mystery to which the monastic life bears such strong witness is the radical, existential solitude of every human person. This solitude—the heart of our emptiness and the center of our fullness, of our true self—is where we encounter the God who is, as Augustine put it in his *Confessions*, "more inward than my innermost and higher than my uppermost" (*interior intimo meo et superior summo meo*).[18] More freely translated, this might be rendered as "more intimate to me than I am to myself." In this interior solitude our hearts uncover our deep yearning to be loved unconditionally, and to love with our whole being. Paradoxically, it is in solitude that we can discover that we are not alone, can come to know a mysterious presence in whom we live and move and have our being (see Acts 17:28), a presence that is known as infinite and infinitely loving, and therefore, in the last analysis, is known as unknowable.

When lived well, Christian monastic life bears vigorous witness to the truth that each of us bears responsibility for our own spiritual life. Merton gave mystical expression to that conviction when he wrote in *Disputed Questions* that each of us must face the full mystery of our lives by taking upon ourselves the lonely, barely comprehensible, and incommunicable task of working our way through the darkness of our own mystery until we discover that our mystery and the mystery God merge into one reality, which is the only reality. In solitude we discover that God lives in us and we in God, not precisely in the way that words seem to suggest (for words have no power to comprehend and express the reality), but in a way that makes words lose their shape, as it were, and become not thoughts, not things, but the unspeakable beating of a Heart within the heart of our own life.[19]

The ideal of the Christian monk is to dedicate his life completely to love, the love of God, humanity, and all creation, and to live out that love beyond all conventional notions of productivity or usefulness. In truth, the monk's task or mission is not to *do* anything. Rather, it is simply to *be* ever more consciously what each of us is called to be and what in reality each of us always and already is: a particular expression of that great mystery of selfless Love that embraces all that is, all that will be. Those who are truly alone and who are conscious of the meaning of their solitude find themselves simply *being* in the hidden ground or mystery of life, in love with all, one with everyone, one with everything.

There is always a danger that in speaking of solitude and celibacy as the skillful means for participating in the mystery of divine love, one will create the impression that the actual experience of solitude and celibacy is one of continuous and ecstatic rapture. The reality, however, is more often one of ordinary, day-to-day existence, sometimes—maybe even often—marked by periods of ennui, emptiness, loneliness, and even repugnance. For one thing, those who choose not to marry and not to flee solitude eventually have to confront their own limitations, failures, and contradictions. Those who marry, of course, are not exempt from this inner work, but attending to the legitimate demands of spouse and family means that the work is accomplished more indirectly and more often without the intense and at times agonizing introspection that is possible for one who has the time and training to reflect and meditate.

It is also true that most monks, at least at the beginning of their monastic life, can only take solitude in small doses. Too much solitude too soon can be terrifying; we simply can't handle it. One of the best descriptions of the extreme challenges of living alone, albeit alone in community, is an account of the experiences of five young men who were novices at St. Hugh's Charterhouse, a Carthusian monastery in West Sussex, England, in the late fifties and early sixties.[20] Four of the five eventually left monastic life, and even though they looked back on their time as Carthusians with gratitude, they recognized that the demands of such intense solitude were more than they were physically and psychologically capable of.

The discoveries made when we listen a little, slow down some, hush up a bit, sit still a moment, bend over and look down into the depths of our being—when we do what is supposed to be done in a monastery—are not very reassuring. We are forced to recognize the self-deception, the posturing, the supine ignorance that has gone into creating this fiction we call the self.[21] But a clear recognition of the problem is also the beginning of a solution, and coming to understand just who we are and how we got that way already shows us what we need to do, and maybe even more, what we need to undergo, if change is to take place. We "learn what it is to be a Christian, to be a sinner in need of redemption rather than a pious man in need of praise."[22]

The self-knowledge possible for those who are free from the daily cares of householders is not to be selfishly hoarded. People look to monks for spiritual guidance precisely because they are given the freedom to devote themselves to the life of the spirit and to share with others the understanding that they have been granted. The interdependence of the monastic and lay life is clearly evident in the Buddhist world, especially in the Theravada tradition, where monks are totally dependent on the laity for their daily sustenance. If the monks become lazy and self-indulgent, more concerned with their material comfort or their status than with their spiritual practice, it is entirely possible that the laity will simply decide to stop supporting them. In the Catholic tradition the motto formulated by the Dominicans—"*Contemplata aliis tradere*," "Handing on to others the fruits of one's contemplation"—expresses the conviction that if monks are freed from worldly care to be able to devote themselves to the life of the spirit, the reason they are afforded this freedom is not just for their own self-improvement but to be of spiritual service to the larger human family.

Celibacy, then, is a practical means to establish the monk in solitude, thereby making possible a more visible witness to the fact that silence and solitude are at the very core of the monastic life, just as fruitful mutuality is intrinsic to the married life. As such, the practice of celibacy itself proclaims—first to the monk himself and then to everyone with whom he comes in contact—the truth that there is at the heart of all human beings an existential solitude, an inescapable aloneness that may be mitigated, but cannot be removed, by anyone or anything, be that friend, spouse, or community. This solitude is at the same time a radical emptiness or openness, a sacred space, for the One who is already *interior intimo meo et superior summo meo.*

By not marrying and by foregoing sexual relationships altogether, those who follow the path of celibacy bear witness to the limits of interpersonal relationships and of the existence and importance of an inner sanctum that is closed to all but God. Indeed, it is in large part by means of his practice of celibacy that the monk is constantly raising—in his own mind and in the minds of others—questions about the deeper meaning of human existence. The monk's life, therefore, is a sign of contradiction and of foolishness to many, at times especially to himself. Yet the monk chooses this particular form of foolishness because he knows on some deep intuitive level that it contains a rich store of wisdom.

As Father Thomas Ryan recounted in his press release,[23] one of the Catholics who participated in Monks of the West spoke of his decision to return to monastic life after having left in order to marry. He recalled his conversation with a group of college students who had come to visit his monastery. The abbot asked him to meet with them for a presentation and discussion about the meaning of monastic life. One of their first questions was, "How can you live without sex? How can you be celibate?" He surprised himself, he said, by the answer that sprang to his lips: "God's a better kisser." He went on to explain that he had been engaged to a woman he deeply loved, but he never lost his desire to seek God and love God as a monk. He recognized that desire is what leads most people to enter into a loving relationship with a spouse, and that the conjugal relationship can become a channel to transcendence, a way to God. But for him, even after he became engaged, there was, as he put it, always a block in the conduit. Celibacy, on the other hand provided him the channel through which the energy of love could flow freely, without stoppage or leaks.

Having said this, it cannot be denied that celibacy also means renunciation, and renunciation is always painful. Even those who do not feel attracted to marriage, who know that they are in a certain sense incapable of marriage, will still experience the pain of loneliness. For some, that pain will be occasional; for some it may be constant, even agonizing. As that precocious Jewish teenager, Anne Frank, noted in her diary, "You can be lonely even when you're loved by many people, since you're still not anybody's 'one and only.'"[24]

It may happen—in fact, one can almost predict with certainty that it *will* happen—that some who have recognized that celibacy is the way they are being called to grow in love will find themselves in a relationship that leads them to think they are now someone's "one and only"—or that they have found their "one and only"—and must therefore change course in order to be true to themselves. It is especially at a time like this that the celibate must recognize and come to accept the reality of his situation. The reward of celibacy is freedom, but the price of celibacy is loneliness, and that price can sometimes be very high.

Chapter 2

One Monk's Path

Learning to Love as a Celibate

With the appearance almost twenty-five years ago of Michael Mott's official biography of Thomas Merton,[1] it became common knowledge that two years before his death in 1968, the most well-known monk in America and one of the foremost spiritual guides of the twentieth century was involved in an intense romantic relationship with a woman who had cared for him when he was a patient in a Louisville hospital. Some were shocked to learn that this Trappist monk, whom they regarded as the most insightful and articulate analyst of religion and society in the Catholic Church, could be swept off his feet by an attractive young nurse. Others, especially those who had been sharply critical of Merton for his forays into political issues and his ever-increasing interest in the spiritual wisdom of other religious traditions, felt that his amorous indiscretions confirmed their suspicions that Merton was moving further and further away from his monastic vocation and even his Catholic faith. But many who read Mott's account of this period of Merton's life admired him all the more for the candor with which he admitted his sexual and emotional struggles, and for his decision to recommit himself to the monastic life with its vow of celibacy.

Thomas Merton became an instant celebrity—in the religious world, at least—when his autobiography, *The Seven Storey Mountain*, appeared in 1948 and became a runaway and enduring bestseller.[2] Many a young Catholic man who decided to enter a monastic or other religious order from the 1950s onward attributed his vocation to the influence of this book.

The content of the books and articles that poured from Merton's pen during the next twenty years gradually shifted from monastic spirituality, more narrowly defined, to an analysis of the principal social and religious questions of the day: racism, militarism, ecumenism, and interreligious dialogue. Merton believed race and peace were the two most urgent issues of our time. He became a strong supporter of the nonviolent civil rights movement, regarding it as the greatest example of Christian faith in action in the social history of the United States. His later interests and writings reflected and developed the sentiments expressed in the opening words of the Second Vatican Council's Pastoral Constitution on the Church in the Modern World (*Gaudium et Spes*):

> The joys and the hopes, the griefs and the anxieties of the men of this age, especially those who are poor or in any way afflicted, these are the joys and hopes, the griefs and anxieties of the followers of Christ. Indeed, nothing genuinely human fails to raise an echo in their hearts.[3]

In the religious sphere, Merton's later writings reveal the strong influence of Zen Buddhism on his spiritual life, an interest that developed through his correspondence and eventual meeting with the Japanese Zen scholar, Daisetz T. Suzuki, the person greatly responsible for introducing Zen Buddhism to the West. But Merton's intellectual and spiritual curiosity was not confined to Buddhism. He read widely in the classics of other religious traditions and carried on an extensive correspondence with Sufi, Confucian, Hindu, and Jewish scholars.[4] He also continued to study the writings of the church fathers and early Cistercian authors, as well as the works of contemporary Christian theologians.

Some critics found Merton's political writings unbecoming of a Catholic monk. They went so far as to suggest that he was becoming a crypto-Communist. Others were scandalized by his acceptance of the spiritual wisdom of Buddhists, Muslims, Jews, and authors who adhered to no particular religion, and believed that he was drifting away from the Catholic Church. But there were many who applauded his outspoken criticism of militarism and racism and his openness to other religious viewpoints. They were grateful for his eloquent prophetic voice calling the Catholic Church to move from a position of isolation and defensiveness to one of engagement with secular society and other religions.

There were those who wanted him to do more. They agreed that his writings were valuable, indeed necessary, but felt he needed to involve himself more actively in the struggle for peace and justice by becoming more socially and politically engaged. They even believed he should take to the streets to protest the war in Vietnam or to march for civil rights. Merton steadfastly resisted their appeal, insisting that it was as a monk—a stay-at-home monk—that he could make his best contribution to needed social change.

Even though Merton recognized, with chagrin, that he enjoyed the notoriety his writing brought him, he never wavered in his conviction that his way of seeking God was the way of solitude. He desired nothing more than to be a monk, more specifically, a hermit monk. At the same time, he struggled to make sense of the solitude he believed was God's will for him. While recognizing how absurd it seemed, he also was convinced that it was a wonderful gift and had enormous possibilities.[5] He also admitted there were times when solitude did not just seem absurd; it profoundly confused and challenged him. In an appendix to his journal he recognized that his life of solitude was a mystery even to himself. "Why do I live alone?" he mused, and then in the same breath responded, "I don't know." He was not even sure he could say that he had chosen solitude. It was, he repeated, an absurd existence, one to which he was not so much "called," but rather, in some mysterious way, "condemned."[6]

We know so much about the private life of this monk for whom solitude was a great and yet exacting blessing because Merton lived his life by writing about it. He began keeping a journal when he was sixteen, and through his frequent entries he observed himself, censured himself, consoled himself, and, above all, discerned the mysterious workings of God in his life. Writing was his way of thinking, praying, and living. "Merton became a monk by writing about becoming a monk," observe the editors of an anthology of all Merton's journals. "He wrote about being lost so that God would find him quickly. He hid himself from the world by fully disclosing himself to it."[7]

Two and a half years before his untimely death—he accidentally electrocuted himself and died while at a monastic conference in Bangkok in 1968—Merton fell in love with a woman he identified in his journals only as "M."[8] Their relationship began less than a year after he took up permanent residence in the hermitage that had been built for him about a mile from the monastery of Gethsemani in Kentucky. He had become a novice in that historic Trappist abbey on December 10, 1941, at the age of twenty-six. From 1955 to 1965 he served as the community's novice master. On August 18, 1965, the abbot appointed a new novice master, and Merton, now fifty, was given permission to become the abbey's first full-time hermit. He was going into the woods, he said, not to find God in the silence and the solitude, but because he believed that was where God wanted to find him.

Less than a year later, in March 1966, Merton was admitted to a hospital in Louisville for back surgery to correct cervical spondylosis, a common degenerative condition of the cervical spine. On March 30, five days after the operation, a student nurse introduced herself to Merton, saying that she had been assigned to take care of him and that she considered it an honor—her way, apparently, of informing him that she knew who he was and thought highly of him. Although Merton was at first annoyed by her intrusion on his time and space (he had been looking forward to using this time to immerse himself in the works of Meister Eckhart), an easy rapport quickly developed between the fifty-one-year-old hermit and a student nurse in her twenties, later identified as Margie Smith by John Howard Griffin, the person originally designated to be Merton's official biographer.[9]

After his return to the hermitage, Merton noted in his journal on April 10, Easter Sunday, that during his time in the hospital he had been cared for by a very friendly and devoted student nurse, a situation, he said, that "livened things up considerably." He then added that they were getting perhaps too friendly by the time she went off on her Easter vacation, but admitted that "her affection—undisguised and frank—was an *enormous* help in bringing me back to life fast."

Being surrounded by all this care and esteem, he said, was "a great indulgence! A huge luxury." What he recognized most of all was that while he was, as he put it, pretty indifferent to his fellow monks and felt no emotional need for community life, he did feel a deep emotional need for feminine companionship and love. What tore him up even more than the operation, he said, was the recognition that he had to live without it.

Merton's journal entries from the time he returned to his hermitage in April 1996 to the end of that year chronicle in minute and at times discomforting detail his love affair with the woman who awakened his emotional need for feminine companionship and love, and at the same time threw his life into a tailspin. He realized that his love for her was "an obsession. And that is bad," and then immediately added, "But it is love." (May 17, 1966). He described the ruses he resorted to in order to phone her, smuggle out love letters and receive hers in return, meet her when he had to return to Louisville to see his doctor or on other business, and even have her join him for a picnic in the woods near his hermitage. Passages expressing his ecstasy at being loved so totally and unconditionally and being able to give love in return are followed by long and painful analyses of his motives along with expressions of dismay at his ability to delude himself.

Merton suspected that his compulsion to chronicle his life without in any way trying to hide his conflicted inner life, would shatter peoples' image of him and might even be found scandalous. He determined that if his journals were to be published, they should be kept under wraps for twenty-five years after his death, though he did consider the possibility of excerpting parts that recounted his relationship with Margie and working them over for publication. He had no intention of bowdlerizing his account of this turning point in his life by, in his words, "keeping the M. business entirely out of sight."

A little more than a year after he met Margie he reflected on all that had transpired and how he had dealt with it in his journal. He insisted that he always wanted to be completely open, both about his mistakes and about his effort to make sense out of his life. The affair with Margie was an important part of it, showing his limitations as well as a side of him that also needed to be known, for it was part of who he was: "My need for love, my loneliness, my inner division, the struggle in which solitude is at once a problem and a 'solution.' And perhaps not a perfect solution either" (May 11, 1967).

What is especially noteworthy about Merton's detailed account of the chaotic summer of 1966 is his clear-sighted recognition that it would be wrong for him to engage in a sexual relationship with Margie not because there is something inherently bad about sex, but because a sexually intimate—even if unconsummated—loving relationship with another person would be incompatible with his option for solitude. Solitude, he was convinced, was his way to become fully human, to seek God, to be of service to his fellow human beings, and, ultimately, to realize fully his call to grow in love and freedom. He knew that for him the solitary, celibate, monastic way of life was the path to wholeness.

Even though he experienced "agonizing fits of loneliness" (August 15, 1966), Merton was convinced that marriage would be an utterly impossible way of life for him. Early in their relationship, he seriously considered the possibility of marrying Margie, going so far as to say that if in the near future the way did open for a married clergy, he would take it (May 9, 1966). But a month later he described a phone call with Margie in which they were talking—foolishly, he noted—about the possibility of his leaving Gethsemani and their getting married. He immediately recognized how preposterous such a conversation was. He simply could not imagine himself in the traditional role of spouse and breadwinner. He also recognized that society would have no place for a well-known former monk and his wife, and he wasn't about to fight to establish a place. But the deeper reason he found their conversation so preposterous was that he really did not want to get married. What he wanted was the life he had vowed (June 12, 1966).

The life Merton had vowed was the monastic life that was constituted by having all things in common, living in chaste celibacy, and giving obedience to the abbot and one's brothers. Having lived that life in community for twenty-five years, he felt himself more and more drawn to "the solitary combat of the desert."[10] On August 13, 1966, he noted that the abbot said he could make his "commitment" or quasi-profession as a hermit. This made him very happy, he wrote, because it meant he could be stabilized, officially and finally, in the hermit state. He wanted to do this for many reasons, but the most important was that there was no other kind of life he was interested in living. About a month later, on September 10, a little more than a year after he began living full-time in the hermitage, he noted in his journal that two days earlier in the presence of his abbot he had made a commitment "to live in solitude for the rest of my life in so far as health may permit." After that, he said, he was at peace and celebrated Mass with great joy.

At the same time, even though he was willing to go forward with this solemn commitment to the solitary life, he knew that his relationship with Margie was something that was not yet fully resolved. In this same entry he described his affection for Margie as "happy, friendly . . . deep and non-obsessed (I hope) and it will last." He felt that he loved her but no longer craved her, and then immediately added, "At least that is how I feel at the moment. But to what extent do I know myself? I know enough to know I may be kidding."

In fact, the craving for affection and physical closeness that at times flummoxed Merton, but also on occasion flooded him with peace during the spring and summer of 1966, abated considerably in the months that followed. His journal entries continue to make frequent reference to his feelings of love for

Margie, but more and more there are statements like "I don't know whether or not I still believe the best of our love was 'from God'" (October 31, 1966). He was much more ready to admit that his relationship with Margie had been a mistake, that he had too easily and too completely yielded to what he now began to think of as a subtle if well-meant seduction. He continued in this same line on the following day when he wrote that "this whole thing with M." was really an attempt to escape the demands of his vocation. "Not consciously, certainly. But a substitution of human love (and erotic love after all) for a special covenant of loneliness and solitude which is the very heart of my vocation."

All throughout this agonizing and bittersweet period of his life Merton struggled to make sense of his love for Margie in light of his conviction that his life would only make sense if lived in solitude. For him, to be a monk, *to be himself*, was to be alone, both in the outward form of his life (being celibate, being a hermit) and in the inner reality of that life. His love affair with Margie Smith led him to question—and ultimately to reaffirm—his commitment to the monastic life and to the celibacy intrinsic to it.[11]

Merton believed that being a monk was the only way for him to reunify the disparate aspects of his life, what he called his "inner division." Over and over again he asked how this ecstatic love for a woman, which he could not deny, could make any sense in the light of his having spent twenty-five years as a monk in community and his recent solemnly expressed resolve to spend the remaining years of his monastic life as a hermit. One thing had suddenly hit him, he said, "that nothing counts except love and that a solitude that is not simply the wide-openness of love and freedom is nothing" (April 14, 1966).

Merton had thought that by taking monastic vows he had gotten control of his sexuality. However, his love for Margie showed him that this was an illusion. After meeting her he regarded the time he had spent in the monastery as "years of rather frantic suppression." By surrendering to what he described as "a kind of inimical womanly wisdom in M. which instinctively seeks out the wound in me that most needs her sweetness, and lavishes all her love upon me there," he felt purified instead of impure, felt that his sexuality had been made real and decent again (May 20, 1966).

Actually, about a half year before he met Margie, Merton was becoming more conscious of his need for feminine solace. On August 17, 1965, he noted that he had received a "very fine letter" from his agent, Naomi Burton, "full of mature, realistic understanding and feminine comfort—the warmth that cannot come from a man and that is so essential." He reflected that psychologically his doubt was based on "this giant, stupid rift in my life, the *refusal* of woman, which is a fault in my chastity (and in the chastity of so many religious!)." He described chastity as his "most radical poverty" and concluded by reflecting that "tragic chastity"—a chastity that realizes itself to be mere loss and fears that death has won—is an ever present possibility for those who make a vow of chastity. It is the risk one has to take to see the other possibility: "the revelation of the Paraclete to the pure heart!"[12]

What prevented the last complete surrender to Margie was precisely his vow and his dedication, "which really come first and make the whole thing absurdly impossible." He always ended up impatient of sex, backing away from domination by it, suspicious of its tyranny, and turning with all his being toward freedom (May 20, 1966).

As Merton continued to reflect on and wrestle with the apparent contradictions between his attraction to Margie and his commitment to the solitary and celibate life, there were times when he began to consider the possibility that these two loves were, in fact, not contradictory but complementary. He wrote that he was not lonely *for* Margie, but in some strange way lonely *with* her, as if she had somehow peacefully become part of his loneliness and of his life that tries to be in God, tries to dwell at the point where life and grace well up out of the unknown (May 2, 1966). Ten days later he reaffirmed this conviction (more probably his longing) that these two loves could coexist by telling himself that his love for Margie was clearly not a contradiction of his solitude but a mysterious part of it (May 12, 1966).

He was still considering the possibility of holding on to both loves in June, when he wrote with a hint of sarcasm and self-deprecation that while this love was a disconcerting, risky, hard-to-handle reality, it was *real*. "It does not fully interfere with or invalidate my solitude (gives it a strange new perspective all right!)" (June 3, 1966). He was steadfast in his conviction, however, that if any kind of selfish exploitation entered into the relationship, it would be wrong, and "could be disastrous for us both" (September 2, 1966).

The desire to live out his solitude while continuing a loving relationship with Margie continued throughout most of the year 1966. In October he wrote that he gave up trying to explain how he could love Margie and at the same time be a hermit. It was simply a fact that his love for solitude and his love for her coexisted. In some paradoxical way his love for Margie actually increased his attraction to the solitary life: "It seems to make me *more* solitary. More detached from 'the world' and more completely independent of it, alien to it" (October 4, 1966). In late November he repeated his conviction that in the depths of his being his love for Margie could coexist with his solitude, but recognized that everything depended on his fidelity to his monastic vocation, which was simply a given, a root fact of his existence that he could not pretend to understand perfectly (November 26, 1966).

At the same time Merton realized that Margie would never be fully able to comprehend or accept his attachment to solitude. He also recognized that she was continuing to hope for a more conventional relationship than Merton was able or willing to enter into. For Merton solitude was not a problem but a vocation, while for her it tended to be *the* problem. An "added cruelty" in Merton's eyes was that she knew that for him it was not only a vocation, but a solution (June 15, 1966). He knew in his heart that his true call was to solitude with God. Having said that, he still found it necessary to add, "And yet I love her. There is nothing for it but to accept the seeming contradiction and make the best of it in trust, without impatience or anxiety, realizing that I can't realistically manipulate things for us to meet etc." (November 16, 1966).

The few entries in the year 1967 that contain references to Margie indicate that Merton had come to realize how dangerous this love affair had been—for both of them—and recognized that the emotional and physical intensity of their relationship had led him to try to convince himself otherwise. At the same time, he was able to affirm God's grace at work, both in the love he had received and given, and in the love he willingly gave up—though not without difficulty and even a kind of regret—for the sake of a greater love.

In April 1967 he was back in Louisville and called Margie from the Brown Hotel. He recalled that they tended to talk as if it were still the same even though it was not. He recognized that one more inexorable step had to be taken to end the relationship. "It is [ended]," he wrote. "But it must be more definitely so. . . . I see again that real loneliness is all that is left for me and I must fully accept it. Nothing else will do" (April 21, 1967).

The next day he noted in his journal that he had made "a sort of perplexed celebration." He had offered Mass for Margie and her fiancé, hoping that they would get back in love again and that they would be happily married. Margie, he said, continued to want to hold on to him sentimentally in some way, but he was convinced that the real love was more or less over between them, though he was sure they would always be fond of each other. "So in a way it is a liberation day—and I have made up my mind to be what I am supposed to be. (Finally!)"

And yet, even though he felt relief at having finally made up his mind, he continued to feel a sense of loss. He could hardly have ended his journal entry for that day more poignantly: "Actually it is a most happy evening—could not be more perfect. . . . Perhaps in a little while I shall go out and stroll around under the trees. And try to tell myself that I am not really sad at all" (April 22, 1967).

On May 10 Merton was again in Louisville to see an allergist, and he called Margie from the airport after seeing off the Jesuit antiwar activist and poet Dan Berrigan. It was almost a year since he and Margie had picnicked in the woods near his hermitage when, as he wrote,

> We ate herring and ham (not very much eating!) and drank our wine and read poems and talked of ourselves and mostly made love and love and love for five hours. And though we had over and over reassured ourselves and agreed that our love would have to continue always chaste and this sacrifice was essential, yet in the end we were getting rather sexy—yet really instead of being all wrong it seemed eminently right. We now love with our whole bodies anyway and I have the complete feel of her being (except her sex) as completely me (May 20, 1966).

Merton described their phone conversation as "sort of heart breaking." Margie said she was going to get married in October, but did not think of it with a lot of joy. She wanted Merton to continue writing to her. "Yes but really I should not," Merton wrote. He again toyed with the idea that they could simply continue to be good friends, sharing what they could reasonably share of each other's news, etc. But then he once again recognized that he was fantasizing: "Probably won't work out that way, though and I came home to lonely woods and desolation" (May 10, 1967).

In July of the same year Merton wrote of having been invited to participate in a fast and added that he had not fasted much at all since last year.

> That business with M. really threw me off my track in a crash. Now I no longer look back on it with longing and desire, but just with embarrassment. It was really a stupid thing—though I recognize that it had a lot of good points because it brought out the things that had to come out and be recognized.

During that period, he said, he lost all serious discipline except for the one thing: solitude. "Keeping to the woods was what saved me" (July 5, 1967).

The final reference to Margie in this penultimate volume of Merton's published journals, which goes up to October 8, 1967, is in an entry he made on July 26:

> I wasted time re-reading bits of this journal—looking again for the M. stuff—so hopeless. . . . I have not had a chance to contact her and—what's the use—don't especially want to. And yet . . . [Merton's own ellipsis] it has been so foolish. I know that what I have to do is work on my meditation, and on the kind of life that people forget exists. And she is no help in that. Yet I felt so much more real when we were in love. And yet too I know how much illusion was in it. (Or at least I can make a good guess!)

The final published volume of Merton's journals covers the period from October 18, 1967, to December 7, 1968, just three days before his death in Bangkok, which occurred, it might be noted, on the twenty-seventh anniversary of his entrance into the novitiate at the Abbey of Gethsemani.

In the course of the last fourteen months of his life Merton made only four brief references to Margie. He called her in November—the first time he had done so, he thought, since June. He remembered it as a "sad sort of call." She was trying to tell him to leave and to "reach out for happiness." He realized there was no way he could tell her that city life would be absolutely meaningless for him and that he could not live happily with a woman—that it would be a disaster for both of them. "Yet I wish I could have a decent talk with her. But what would be the use?" (November 12, 1967).[13]

In early December he received two letters from a man and a woman teaching at a university in England to thank him for "Notes on Love," an article he had written for the journal *Frontier*.[14] He reflected that if his notes "helped two people to love each other better and with more trust in love's truth, then all that happened between me and M. was worthwhile." He then mentioned that he had written her a couple days earlier but had run out of things to say because she was still thinking he should leave Gethsemani, "But that is no longer reasonable" (December 2, 1967).

Shortly before Christmas he received a card from Margie and remarked that he had thought of her—"almost saw her it was so vivid"—on the day the card was mailed. He admitted that he felt less real without "our constant communication, our sense of being in communion (so intense last year)," and reflected on the contrast with "the drab, futile silences of this artificial life, with all its tensions and its pretences." But he was realistic enough to recognize that "it would be worse somewhere else. And marriage, for me, would be terrible! Anyway, that's all over."

But once again the ambiguity of it all rose to the surface. In the very next paragraph he wrote, "Yet this afternoon I wondered if I'd really missed the point of life after all. A dreadful thought!" (December 23, 1967).

Merton's final reference to Margie in his journals could hardly be more definitive or more dramatic. At the beginning of the entry he noted, "I have been three years officially in this hermitage." And then, "Today, among other things, I burned M.'s letters. Incredible stupidity in 1966! I did not even glance at any one of them. High hot flames of the pine branches in the sun!" (August 20, 1967).

What is especially striking in Merton's attempts to analyze and understand what was going on in his relationship with Margie—beyond the sheer brilliance (to say nothing of the sheer volume!) of his record of this love affair and the emotional turmoil it caused—is how often he returned to the themes of solitude, freedom, and love—the "special covenant with loneliness and solitude," the reality that comprised the very core of his monastic calling and to which he recommitted himself with full knowledge of how costly and painful such a commitment had been and would continue to be.

Merton's relationship with Margie began just a year after he had been able to realize his dream of living as a hermit, and just at the time he was working on a preface for the Japanese edition of *Thoughts in Solitude*,[15] an essay that contains some of his most mature, theologically profound, and poetic reflections on the meaning of solitude.[16] John Howard Griffin says that he lent Margie the manuscript in an effort to help her understand his hermit vocation,[17] though Merton himself makes no mention of this in his journal.

Again and again Merton expressed his inability to give up solitude even as he admitted and struggled with the intensity of his affection for Margie and hers for him. Even when their relationship had reached its passionate apogee, he could say, "I am a solitary and that's that. Sure, I love M. but [that] can never interfere with my main purpose in life—and that is that" (May 23, 1966). He would allow nothing to get in the way of his aloneness, his freedom, his being without care, unconnected, with nothing to gain and nothing to lose.

He also recognized that even when they were most intimate with one another, they did not meet completely in their love. It was partial, not whole. Each tried, as he put it, to envelop the whole self of the other, and then his own ambiguities would come into play. "My deepest self evades this and is jealous of absolute freedom and solitude" (May 24, 1966).

In June 1966, the day after the abbot returned to Gethsemani from what appears to have been a fairly lengthy absence, Merton decided the best thing was to own up and face Dom James before he summoned him in. However, he later added the following parenthetical comment in his journal: "(about the phone calls *only!*)," thereby admitting that he had been rather selective—to say the least!—when he told his abbot what was happening in his relationship with Margie. He noted that the abbot "tried to be understanding to some extent—his only solution was of course 'a complete break.'" Dom James suggested that a contributing factor in the development of this relationship might have been the solitude of the hermitage and proposed that, for his own spiritual and emotional health, Merton return to the monastery (June 14, 1966).

In an undated letter to Abbot James that was most likely written shortly after this meeting, Merton clearly stated how central solitude and freedom were to his monastic calling and his true self. From every point of view, he said, it would be wrong for him to return even partially to the community life. He did not think his failures were a reason for abandoning solitude but for continuing in it with renewed resolution and with greater understanding, prudence, and reliance on prayer. "Never think that I take the solitary life lightly. I cannot take it lightly. It is the most important thing in my existence and I have to cling to it with all my power."[18]

To all extents and purposes Merton's love affair with Margie came to an end in the summer of 1967. In December of that year, and then again in May 1968, Merton invited prioresses of contemplative communities to Gethsemani for what he called a "searching retreat," a time to come together in a quiet place to think and to pray. His conferences and conversations were recorded, transcribed, and published under the title *The Springs of Contemplation*. Given the fact that he had ended his relationship with Margie Smith less than a year earlier, it is especially interesting to read his response to one of the prioresses who, during the course of the May 1968 retreat, asked him to comment on virginity, remarking that some of the young people coming to monastic life wanted to be virginal, but rejected the notion that it was a higher state of life.

Merton replied that there was a real freedom in simply not being involved in sex. "I don't know how to explain it," he said, "it's just a more free kind of life." Obviously speaking from experience—though not explicitly referring to his relationship with Margie—he went on to say that when people are involved in a sexual situation, they can get very caught up in it. "Anybody who's ever been deeply in love knows what it's like. If it's too involved"—as mine certainly was, he must have been thinking—"there's real slavery, because you can't think of anything else. And there's no question of praying."

Merton noted that he was speaking about a passionate relationship outside of marriage. And then, once again obviously speaking from personal experience, he said,

> It takes all you've got. There's no time or energy for anything else. It seems to me that anyone who knows what that involves would be delighted to be released from it. To feel free again, to be able to pray if you want, to have a sense of being all one, are things we value in our life.

"Virginity," he concluded, "is a certain way of living with your body so that it isn't a hindrance to you. You are free to pray and study and work."[19]

To feel free again, free to pray and study and work. To have a sense of being all one, that—along with the loneliness that is its inevitable companion—is how Merton experienced and spoke about celibacy. He was fully aware, painfully aware, that embracing celibacy is no guarantee that one's life will be free of crisis, doubt, and pain. But he showed by his own experience that one can come to a fuller and deeper appreciation of how precious and worthwhile celibacy can be, precisely because one has struggled through a period of intense confusion brought on by falling in love and being loved by another person.

There are those, of course, who in all honesty—and they may well be correct—interpret an experience of falling in love as a sign that they chose wrongly when they chose celibacy, that celibacy was not the way for them to realize their humanity and find their way back to God. Merton, however, did not come to that conclusion. No matter how strong the passion, how exhilarating the ecstasy, how dangerous the circumstances of his love for Margie, he persevered in his conviction that his way to freedom and wholeness was through solitude and celibacy. At times this realization brought him peace; at times it tore him apart and brought him to the brink of despair. But the conviction never left him.

Even though Merton told the prioress who questioned him about the meaning of virginity that there was "no question of praying" if one was involved in a passionate relationship, his own journals make it clear that he did continue to pray and meditate. Early on in his relationship with Margie he noted that whatever else he did, reading and meditation remained important to keep in perfect touch with reality, to avoid the divisions created by yearning and speculation (May 10, 1966). In June he reflected that the crucial point was to offer oneself to God as a sacrifice of obedience in faith, the God, he said, who was "begetting His love in me (which has never stopped)" (June 30, 1966). On another occasion he noted that he only recovered a "real awake 'mindfulness'" after about three hours of reading. His other state was of an anxious, disoriented consciousness in which he made erratic and desperate acts "calling on God, trying to recover orientation, thinking of M., questioning self, fearing consequences of imprudence, etc." (July 14, 1966).

Merton also found strength and insight from his growing familiarity with Buddhist teachings and practices. "Today—back to meditation on the *Dhammapada*—something sound to support me when everything else is quicksand" (April 24, 1966).[20] He began an entry in mid-June noting that "'In order to untie a knot you must first find out how the knot was tied' (Buddha)" (June 15, 1966). In July he referred to his reading of Nyanaponika Thera's treatise on Buddhist meditation, which he found to be excellent. Noting that it dealt with the basics, he commented, "There is a healthy empiricism in Buddhist ascesis!" (July 20, 1966).

The journal entries in which Merton chronicled his love affair with Margie at times read like pitiable attempts of a man going through a midlife crisis who is trying to convince himself that his infatuation for a woman half his age is actually a sign that he is finally discovering the truth about himself, the truth about life, even the truth about God. But one cannot read very far without recognizing that Merton was painfully conscious of his ability to deceive himself. He was aware of how stupidly he had acted, aware that others were disappointed in him, and ultimately aware of his own weakness. What he did, however, was to apply to himself the advice he had given his novices years earlier when lecturing to them on Cassian: "It is for us, with St. Paul, to learn the lesson that God's grace is sufficient, and that holiness demands the acceptance of our human frailty and the willingness to face trial with patience. This is the way of realism and of humility."[21]

The celibacy to which Merton recommitted himself might well be described as a celibacy that had been demythologized. He spoke of his desire for the celibate monastic life more in terms of a natural disposition than as a higher calling or "charism," recognizing that he was by nature predisposed to lead an interior life, both intellectually and spiritually. To do that he needed the freedom that monastic celibacy makes possible. Although he insisted that he was totally unsuited for marriage and had no desire to live as a married man, he never spoke about marriage as an inferior way to follow Christ, or about his wish to live out his days as a celibate as a higher calling. But while his celibacy was demythologized, he took it with utmost seriousness, struggling to find the appropriate way to love real people, and in particular a real woman, without becoming attached and without using others to fulfill his own needs for affection and affirmation.

Merton recognized that his relationship with Margie had to change, indeed had to be terminated. For one thing, it was irresponsible of him to do or say anything that would keep alive her hope that he might one day leave Gethsemani to marry her. He also recognized how improper it would be to allow her to think she could continue to rely on him for emotional support even if she married someone else. But he never suggested that she should enter a convent so that, like a modern day Abelard and Heloise, they could prolong and deepen their spiritual friendship. He wanted her to marry and to find happiness—and holiness—as a married woman and mother. His way was not marriage, but hers was, and they both needed to walk the path that suited their natures, the different paths to which God was calling them through their different characters and temperaments.

Chapter 3

Different Paths, One Destination

A Catholic Approach
to Celibacy and Marriage

Celibacy for Roman Catholics has been mythologized by a long tradition of thinking and speaking of it as a more difficult, higher, and surer path to holiness. This point of view may owe more to a particular way of reading some passages in the First Letter of Saint Paul to the Corinthians than to the actual experience of life as a celibate. This is not to say that celibacy is without challenges and difficulties, but rather to state an obvious but often overlooked home truth: marriage is an incredibly demanding vocation and not the low road for those who are too weak or too selfish to live celibately.

Contemporary Catholic teaching on marriage is unambiguous in its assertion that marriage is an efficacious path to holiness. The Second Vatican Council's Constitution on the Church in the Modern World (*Gaudium et Spes*) describes authentic married love as "caught up into divine love and governed and enriched by Christ's redeeming power and the saving activity of the Church." The council fathers go on to say that by virtue of the sacrament of matrimony married couples are "penetrated with the spirit of Christ, which suffuses their whole lives with faith, hope and charity." Accordingly, it is by virtue of their marriage—and not in spite of it—that husband and wife "increasingly advance the perfection of their own personalities, as well as their mutual sanctification, and hence contribute jointly to the glory of God" (48).

The understanding of marriage set out in this document is clearly positive, but there is still some reluctance to accord married people the same status given to those who "consecrate" their lives to God through the vows of poverty, chastity, and obedience. *Gaudium et Spes* says that "Christian spouses have a special sacrament by which they are fortified and receive a kind of consecration in the duties and dignity of their state" (48). The expression "a kind of consecration" (*et veluti consecrantur*—literally, "and are, as it were, consecrated") is taken from the 1930 encyclical of Pope Pius XI on marriage, *Casti Connubii*,[1] in which he writes, "By such a sacrament [matrimony] they will be strengthened, sanctified and in a manner consecrated" (41). It is a bit puzzling, to say the least, that these official documents speak of the lives of those who vow celibacy as "consecrated," while the lives of those who vow to remain faithful to one another in marriage and whose commitment is regarded as a sacrament—an *efficacious* sign of God's sanctifying presence according to Catholic theology—are said to be only "in a manner consecrated."

Contemporary Catholic teaching regards celibacy and marriage as different but complementary ways of living out one's sexuality, either of which can be the way to put on the mind of Christ (see Phil 2:5) and thus walk the holy path that leads to God. Although official documents still reserve the expression "consecrated life" to men and women who have taken vows of chastity, poverty, and obedience, many Catholics would feel uncomfortable referring to celibacy as the "objectively higher state"—though one can still find that kind of language in contemporary writings. The willingness of the church to speak of marriage as an authentic path to holiness has, in turn, prompted a reconsideration of those passages of Scripture that once were used as "proof texts" to show that celibacy was to be accorded a dignity greater than that given to marriage.

At the same time, it must be admitted that old habits of thought die hard. The Roman Catholic Church continues to regard with favor the wishes of a married couple who mutually agree to live celibately, whether by continuing to live together as brother and sister or by becoming vowed members of a religious order. A person who has taken the vow of celibate chastity, however, and wishes to be dispensed of his vow in order to marry, would be regarded as having failed. If that person had been ordained to the priesthood after having vowed chastity on becoming a monk or a member of a religious order, it is now unlikely that his petition for a dispensation to marry would be granted.

The Catholic Church's list of saints is also indicative of the degree to which celibacy has been viewed more positively than marriage. Rare is the canonized saint who had been married, and those married women whose sanctity was recognized by the church were most often canonized because of their virtuous lives as widows. Part of the reason for this state of affairs is that the long and costly process of investigation that precedes canonization needs the backing of an organization like a religious order with the desire and the resources to see its founder elevated to the ranks of the saints. The fact remains, however, that there is, as yet, no saint who was canonized *because* he or she was a loving spouse. On October 21, 2001, Pope John Paul II did beatify a twentieth-century Italian couple, Luigi and Maria Beltrame Quattrocchi.[2] It was the first time in the history of the Catholic Church that a husband and wife were elevated together to the rank of "blessed." However, one of the reasons for their beatification was that they exhibited "heroic holiness" by taking a vow of celibacy after twenty years of marriage and four children.

While a certain ambiguity may remain regarding the relative value of celibacy and marriage, contemporary Catholic teaching is strong in its insistence that the erotic love that draws couples together can be a true path to holiness. In his first encyclical letter, *Deus caritas est*, Pope Benedict XVI reflected on the complementary natures of *eros*, the love of attraction or desire, and *agape*, selfless love. Divine love—and the human love in which divine love is reflected—is not just that selfless devotion that the Greek New Testament calls *agape*; it is also passionate love, *eros*. While noting that the word *eros* never occurs in the New Testament, Pope Benedict insists, "God loves, and his love may certainly be called *eros*, yet it is also totally *agape*" (9).[3]

The reason Pope Benedict says that God's love may be called *eros* is because the people of Israel and the followers of Jesus experienced God's love as a love that was totally giving—*agape*—and at the same time intensely passionate, even though they did not use the word *eros* to describe the passionate quality of God's love. Because God's love is both *eros* and *agape*, human love also begins with *eros* and blossoms into *agape*. In Benedict's words,

> Even if *eros* is at first mainly covetous and ascending, [fascinated by] the great promise of happiness, [when it draws] near to the other, it [becomes] less and less concerned with itself [and] increasingly seeks the happiness of the other. . . . The element of *agape* thus enters into this love, for otherwise *eros* is impoverished and even loses its own nature. On the other hand, [we] cannot live by . . . descending love alone. [We] cannot always give. [We] must also receive. Anyone who wishes to give love must also receive love as a gift. (7)

The most explicit teaching of Jesus on celibacy is to be found in the nineteenth chapter of the Gospel of Saint Matthew. There Jesus concludes his response to the Pharisee's question about the legitimacy of divorce by saying "It was because you were so hard-hearted that Moses allowed you to divorce your wives, but at the beginning it was not so. And I say to you, whoever divorces his wife, except for unchastity, and marries another commits adultery" (19:8-9).

In response to these demanding words of Jesus, his dispirited disciples can only sigh, "If such is the case of a man with his wife, it is better not to marry" (19:10), to which Jesus replies,

> Not everyone can accept this teaching, but only those to whom it is given. For there are eunuchs who have been so from birth, and there are eunuchs who have been made eunuchs by others, and there are eunuchs who have made themselves eunuchs for the sake of the kingdom of heaven. Let anyone accept this who can. (19:11-12)

The key to understanding these words of Jesus lies in the meaning of the challenge, "Let anyone accept this who can." The

Greek word for "accept"—*chōrein*, from the substantive *chōros*, a space or place—literally means "to make room for." The meaning of Jesus' question might thus be paraphrased, "Can you understand what is being said to you?" What the disciples of Jesus are being asked to accept—to make room for, to understand—is not a tough teaching about the necessity and difficulty of celibacy, but rather the insistence of Jesus that the marriage bond is indissoluble, "except for unchastity."[4]

Jesus' saying on eunuchs has to be understood in the light of what he had just said about marriage. The disciples, in dismay at the thought of a marriage from which there is virtually no way out, are comforted with the assurance that there is another way—an easier but equally acceptable way—to enter the kingdom. You do not have to get married—and stay married—to experience the fullness of God's love and to love God and neighbor in return. Eunuchs—whether they were born that way, made that way by others, or freely chose that way of life—can also be signs of the kingdom of heaven.

If this is not the way this passage of Scripture has usually been understood, the reason, in large measure, can be attributed to the fact that biblical interpretation—in the Catholic Church at least—used to be the exclusive domain of celibate men. They defended their way of life not simply as another way, but as a better way, and interpreted the words of Jesus as a vindication of their superior position in the church.

If we look at the passage carefully, however, it is clear that the primary focus of the passage is on marriage. The purpose of Jesus' instruction is to insist that human marriage is a reflection of the covenant God entered into with the people of Israel, a covenant that had been described by the prophets in terms of marriage.

The nuptial character of God's relationship with the people of Israel was especially highlighted by the prophet Hosea who had God say to the people, "I will take you for my wife forever; I will take you for my wife in righteousness and in justice, in steadfast love, and in mercy. I will take you for my wife in faithfulness: and you shall know the LORD" (2:19-20). Generations later the

Prophet Ezekiel provided an especially poignant account of God's conjugal relationship with Israel. God had rescued Israel when she was like a cast-off newborn baby. God raised her, betrothed her, only to be betrayed by her adulterous—that is, idolatrous—behavior, which led to her downfall and brought upon her the scorn of all her neighbors. But rather than divorcing her, God renewed his covenant with her: "I will establish my covenant with you, and you shall know that I am the LORD, in order that you may remember and be confounded, and never open your mouth again because of your shame, when I forgive you all that you have done, says the LORD GOD" (16:62f.)

Drawing on this prophetic tradition, Jesus responds to the disciples' question about the legitimacy of divorce by insisting that just as God's nuptial covenant with the people of Israel is permanent and irrevocable, human marriage must also be permanent. The disciples are dismayed by such a stringent demand and wonder if more is being asked of them than they are capable of. In response to their anxiety, the evangelist Matthew inserts the saying about eunuchs, that is, men who are incapable of marriage. The logical implication would appear to be that even though celibacy is a less demanding vocation than marriage, those who cannot or choose not to marry—provided they so choose not for personal gain but "for the sake of the kingdom of heaven"—are also invited to be citizens and signs of the kingdom that Jesus has come to proclaim.

When we move from the Gospels to the letters of Paul, the text that has probably had the greatest impact on the way Catholics thought, and to some degree continue to think, about celibacy is the seventh chapter of the First Letter to the Corinthians. In this chapter, as in much of the rest of the letter, Paul is responding to questions put to him by the Christian community in Corinth. Regarding his treatment of marriage and celibacy, he specifically says he is responding "to the matters about which you wrote: 'It is well for a man not to touch a woman'" (7:1).

What exactly is Paul saying in this verse? Is he simply repeating an axiom on which the Corinthians wanted Paul to give an opinion, or is he beginning his response with a statement of what he believes to be true? In either case, what exactly is the meaning of "it is well" (*kalon estin*)?

Some would argue that "it is well" actually means "it is better" on the grounds that the Greek word for "good" (*kalon*) is also used in the New Testament to mean "better." Jesus, for example, says, "If your hand or your foot causes you to stumble, cut it off and throw it away; it is better (*kalon*) for you to enter life maimed or lame than to have two hands or two feet and to be thrown into the eternal fire" (Matt 18:8); or, "If any of you put a stumbling-block before one of these little ones who believe in me, it would be better (*kalon*) for you if a great millstone were hung around your neck and you were thrown into the sea" (Mark 9:42).

However, Paul does make use of the comparative form of *kalon*, namely *mallon*, to mean "better." Just a little further on in this same letter to the Corinthians he says, "But I have made no use of any of these rights, nor am I writing this so that they may be applied in my case. Indeed, I would rather die [literally, it would be better (*mallon*) for me to die] than that" (1 Cor 9:15).

The questions the Christians in Corinth addressed to Paul regarding sex and marriage seem to have come from an element within the community that insisted on celibacy as the ideal if not the only path to spiritual maturity. It is possible that they were inspired not only by the example of Jesus and Paul, but also by such ascetics as the Essenes, the Pythagoreans, or the Therapeutae, contemporary spiritual fraternities (they were mainly, though not exclusively, male associations) from the Jewish and Greek world whose members believed the renunciation of property and sexual activity was integral to the pursuit of spiritual perfection.

If, therefore, the phrase "It is well for a man not to touch a woman" is what the Corinthians were saying, they probably did mean "It is better . . ." On the other hand, if Paul is prefacing his response with a statement of his belief about the relative value of marriage and celibacy, then it probably simply means "It is well" or "It is good," since what Paul will go on to say does not indicate that he regarded celibacy *in itself* as better than marriage.

Paul's response, "But because of cases of sexually immorality, each man should have his own wife and each woman her own husband" (7:2), could give the impression that he regards marriage as the lesser of two evils, a way to channel sexual energy that could otherwise lead one to engage in lewd and abusive behavior. This impression is reinforced by his statement a little further on, "It is better to marry than to be aflame with passion" (7:9). However, it must be remembered that Paul's questioners were challenging him. In order to make his point, he had to come up with an argument calculated to convince his adversaries that marriage was an acceptable option for followers of Jesus Christ.

Paul goes on to say that he is not commanding the Christian people of Corinth to marry. Marriage is permitted, but it is not imposed. At the same time he clearly states, "I wish that all were as I myself am. But each has a particular gift (*charisma*) from God" (7:7); literally, "each one has his own gift of God."

On the basis of Paul's words, defenders of celibacy have argued that the renunciation of marriage is a higher, a better, or at least a "special" calling because it is a "charism" or gift from God. However, Paul does not say or even imply that marriage is not equally a gift from God. Celibacy and marriage are different ways of life, different responses to Jesus' call to discipleship, but marriage lived as an expression of a transformed life, as a sacrament of *agape*, is also a charism, a gift from God to be received with gratitude. Paul makes that very clear when he says, "one having one kind [of gift] and another a different one" (7:7); literally, "one thus, another thus."

Using "charism" language to speak about celibacy, but not about marriage, is problematic for at least two reasons. In the first place, it reinforces the all too prevalent myth about celibacy, namely, that it is a special calling from God, while marriage is simply the default option for people who are not guided by spiritual values or concerns. According to this view, celibate people have received a special gift, a divine calling, and have responded to it. Therefore, they are obviously superior to all those ordinary laypeople who just "got married."

Identifying celibacy as a charism is problematic on other grounds. If I, as a celibate, regard my way of life as a special gift from God, not only am I tempted think of myself as superior, I can easily dispense myself from the discipline necessary to live this life well. My rationale will be that celibacy, after all, has nothing to do with human achievement; it is a grace, a freely given gift. Furthermore, when loneliness makes itself felt with special intensity, or if the "right" person comes into my life, it will be all too easy to conclude that I must have been mistaken when I believed that I had received the charism of celibacy, because the desire to live with another person—or even the seemingly irresistible urge to have sex—is an obvious sign that I never received or no longer have the charism.

But even though Paul did not claim that celibacy is intrinsically superior to marriage, it cannot be denied that he would prefer the unmarried members of the Corinthian community to remain single. He writes, "He who marries his fiancée does well (*kalōs*); and he who refrains from marriage will do better (*kreisson*)" (7:38). A little further on he says about widows, "She is free to marry anyone she wishes, only in the Lord. But in my judgment she is more blessed (*machariōtera*) if she remains as she is" (7:40).

The reason Paul encouraged celibacy in the Corinthian community is that his teaching was given in the context of a generalized belief that the parousia, the end of this world as we know it and the full manifestation of Christ as the Lord of the universe, was imminent. "The appointed time has grown short . . . the present form of this world is passing away" (7:29, 31) is the way he put it. In his mind, it is of utmost importance that the followers of Jesus prepare for his return—or better, his appearance—in glory by lives of concentrated and undistracted watching and praying.

Paul was not alone in believing that the end of the world as we know it was near. It was the common conviction of first-generation Christians. Since time was running out, what sense did it make to begin a family or to be concerned about accumulating possessions and occupying oneself in worldly affairs (see

7:30-31)? In such a situation, it is "better" not to marry, and one who does not marry will be "more blessed," that is, happier—or, as we might say today, less stressed—because she will be freed of the cares and anxieties that are an inevitable component of married life. Consequently, she will be able to devote all her attention to preparing for the imminent appearance of the Lord in glory.

What Paul is saying, in other words, is that in the short period of time that is left before the parousia, he would like peoples' lives to be as uncomplicated as possible. Celibacy allows one to focus on preparing to meet the Lord when he appears in glory in a way that is simply not possible for those who are married. We might go so far as to say that celibacy is "better" than marriage because it is easier; the widow who does not remarry will be "more blessed" because she will be freer.

For a Christian the celibate life bears witness to the kingdom proclaimed by Jesus when it is practiced as a path to self-transcendence, as a way of dying to self with Christ in order to be raised to new life with him. The word "when" is crucial. Being celibate does not necessarily lead one to a life of self-transcending love, the kind of love the Scriptures refer to as *agape*. In fact, it can be chosen or lived out precisely because it offers one more freedom than is possible to one who is married or, for that matter, in any committed and exclusive relationship.

Women, on whom marriage has traditionally imposed the larger share of the drudgery of housekeeping and the incessant demands of parenthood, have especially understood the benefits of what is sometimes termed the "new celibacy." On January 16, 2007, the *New York Times* reported on the growing number of American women who are living without a spouse: 51 percent in 2005, up from 49 percent in 2000 and 35 percent in 1950.[5]

Several factors, it seems, are driving this statistical shift. Women are marrying later and live longer than their husbands. After a divorce or after the death of their spouse, they are more likely than men to delay remarriage, sometimes delighting in their newfound freedom. One divorced woman who had been married for thirty-three years said, "I'm in a place in my life where I'm comfortable. I can do what I want, when I want, with whom I want. I was a wife and a mother. I don't feel like I need to do that again." Another woman whose marriage ended after thirty years said, "The benefits were completely unforeseen for me, the free time, the amount of time I get to spend with friends, the time I have alone, which I value tremendously, the flexibility in terms of work, travel and cultural events."

As these women know very well, the life of a wife and mother is considerably more demanding than that of a single person—as is the life of a husband and father, though very often not to the same degree. For both husband and wife there are first of all the challenges of living in an intimate relationship with one person over an extended period of time. It can happen that the very qualities that spouses once found so attractive in one another become almost unbearable irritations. In the heat of passion it is easy to overlook little quirks and foibles; as passion cools, they can become sources of extreme irritation and even disgust.

And then follow the hardships that inevitably arise when children enter the picture: nights without sleep; social and recreational activities curtailed by the demands of child care; anguish caused by sickness, injury, or even death; the terrible threes; adolescent rebellion; disagreements about how or even whether to discipline a child who has misbehaved. Rare is the day when a married person is not faced with a situation that calls for surrendering one's own agenda in order to respond to the needs of a spouse or a child. If holiness consists in dying to self in order to live for the other with whom Christ identifies himself, it is hard to imagine a life situation that provides as many opportunities for *agape* as married family life.

What hurts some married people very deeply is the recognition that having entered into marriage with the expectation that a permanent commitment to each other would deepen their sense of being one, they experience a painful and perhaps even increasing distance from their partner. They know what it means to be one flesh, but they sense that they are far from becoming one mind and one spirit.

A reporter for National Public Radio reflected on this sadness as he described pulling together an hour of love-themed dinner music for his niece's wedding reception. From the start, he had set strict guidelines: No heartbreak or infidelity. Nothing unnerving, angry, or lusty. It all seemed easy enough, given the countless number of songs that pay tribute to love between two people. They must have *something* to say about the kind that lasts forever.

But so many of those love songs, he discovered, were still searching for happiness, or dwelling on mistakes made along the way. Try as he might to produce an upbeat wedding mix, in its finished form it contained, he said, "more than a slight whiff of agony and hardship, decay and death." (One can almost imagine the Buddhist listener nodding compassionately and murmuring, "But, of course, of course . . .")

He concluded his report by musing:

> On my niece's wedding night, my bittersweet mix-tape masterpiece played faintly over the din of forks hitting wine glasses. Eager to have it heard by the bride and groom's distant cousins and high-school classmates, I brought copies for anyone willing to take it. My hope is that it reached someone—that he or she drove home next to a sleeping passenger, put it on, listened intently, and sobbed audibly under the night sky.[6]

Those who have opted for celibacy are delivered from the pain of having an intimate relationship turn sour. They also enjoy a remarkable degree of freedom and independence. They are not tied down the way married people are, but can more easily drop everything and head off to a place of peace and quiet. They have much more control over their schedules, the way they organize their living space, their personal life.

There is a flip side to this, of course. Peace and quiet can produce a sense of isolation, a feeling that no one cares or is interested in you. This is especially true for those celibates who live alone, but those who live in community also have to deal with loneliness and a sense of being ignored or taken for granted. It is easy at times like that to engage in self-pity and to think that a spouse or a partner would change everything, that I would never have to be lonely again because there would always be someone there who loved me and was ready to respond to my every need for intimacy and affirmation.

Married people, of course, will be the first to point out that feelings of loneliness and isolation are also part of their experience. One can easily imagine that for them the experience is even more painful than it is for the celibate. At some point in their marriage some spouses may begin to feel that their conversations with one another have become mere formalities. They feel that they are growing apart; but even if they know why, they feel unable or, for reasons they cannot understand, unwilling to change course. They would do anything to rekindle the love they felt for one another when they began their married life, but they don't where to begin. Loneliness is always painful, but loneliness *à deux* has to be hell, not exactly the kind of hell Jean Paul Sartre had in mind when he penned his celebrated dictum, *"L'enfer, c'est les autres,"* "Hell is other people," but hell nonetheless.

There is little doubt that Catholicism's positive regard for marriage as a spiritual path differs considerably from Buddhist teaching and practice. At the same time, there are nuances within Buddhism regarding the necessity of celibacy to be delivered from the cycle of rebirth. Some would say that to achieve the stages of the Buddhist path, celibacy is not essential; it is simply an aid. The main objective of the path to nirvana is to abandon one's desire for sensory pleasure—not sensory pleasure itself, but the desire for it. Such abandonment is achieved on the basis of morality, meditation, and wisdom.

There are nuances within the Catholic tradition as well. As much as Catholic theology—contemporary Catholic theology, that is—pays tribute to marriage as an authentic path to holiness, it still has to reckon with the words of Jesus that "in the resurrection they neither marry nor are given in marriage, but are like angels in heaven" (Matt 22:30). Jesus spoke these words in answer to the Sadducees, a Jewish sect that denied the resurrection, who had presented him with the hypothetical case of a woman whose seven husbands had all died. In a classical *reductio ad absurdum* they had asked him, "In the resurrection, then, whose wife of the seven will she be? For all of them had married her" (Matt 22:28). On the basis of Jesus' answer, one would have to say that while Christianity views marriage as a valid way to spiritual growth and maturity, it is not part of the spiritually perfected existence that Christians term the resurrection or the risen life.

Buddhist monks, especially those of the Theravada tradition, would hold that while married people are also called to walk a spiritual path, this path cannot be completed without celibacy. Because of the legitimate demands of married life, spiritual practice is partial and piecemeal. The Buddhist monk regards celibacy as a more effective means to move toward the one-pointed stillness (*samadhi*) that leads to insight and the peace and happiness that flow from it. A householder can attain to the first stage—a glimpse of nirvana—and possibly the second stage. But the remaining stages cannot be attained unless one is celibate.

From a Buddhist point of view, sexuality is not necessarily seen as a block to final liberation. Rather, one who is fully liberated would be totally uninterested in sex, having gone beyond sexual desire. In order to arrive at that stage, however, it is necessary to devote oneself to a life that helps one avoid those situations that would increase attachment to sensual pleasure and to dedicate oneself to cultivating the life of the spirit. It is to this end that the Buddha and Benedict formulated their monastic rules.

Chapter 4

The Celibate Path for Monks

Buddhist and Catholic Teachings and Practices

The two major schools within Buddhism, Theravada ("Way of the Elders") and Mahayana ("Great Vehicle"), are probably best understood as different expressions, many of them culturally conditioned, of the same teaching of the historical Buddha. Mahayana Buddhism developed in China, Korea, and Japan, while Theravada flourished in Sri Lanka, Myanmar, Thailand, and Cambodia. As James Wiseman points out, the difference between these two branches has at times been expressed in the simplistic assertion that "the Theravada ideal is a self-centered quest for Nirvana on the part of an *Arhat* whereas Mahayana is characterized by the *Bodhisattva's* altruistic desire to bring all beings to enlightenment."[1] Even though the Buddhist movement spread over a wide geographical area and was shaped by different cultures, Theravada and Mahayana Buddhists agree upon and practice the core teachings of the Buddha. The major area of difference is over rules for the monastic way of life, which, in its celibate, mendicant form, has been kept alive to a greater degree in Southeast Asia, where the Theravada school is dominant.

Theravada monks and nuns (*bhikkhus* and *bhikkhunis*) attribute the discipline (*Vinaya*) they follow to the historical Buddha, Siddhartha Gautama (ca. 563-483 B.C.E.). Tradition has it that during the first years of the monastic community (*sangha*) there was no Vinaya because the Buddha was among his disciples, teaching them by word and example. But as the sangha grew,

welcoming newcomers and becoming a large movement, many
bhikkhus ended up living in places where they seldom or perhaps never saw the Buddha. It became necessary to have a written code to guide their way of life and to respond to infractions
as they arose.

What is distinctive about the basic rules of conduct for bhikkhus and bhikkhunis that comprise the first part of the Vinaya
is that every rule the Buddha set down—including those that
deal with sexual behavior—was made in response to a specific
transgression. When a member of the sangha would act in an
unskillful way and the offence came to the attention of the Buddha, he would make a judgment on the case. This judgment was
given in the form of a rule that then became binding on all the
members.

These rules, along with the discussions that serve as a commentary on them, are preserved in a number of Vinaya texts. In
the Theravada tradition the core is the set of 227 rules (311 for
bhikkhunis) called *Patimokkha* (Pali) or *Pratimoksha* (Sanskrit).[2]
This body of monastic rules exists in three different recensions,
each one coming from a different Buddhist school. Scholarly
work on these recensions has shown that while there is significant divergence in regard to the minor rules—those dealing with
monastic etiquette, for example—there is very little discrepancy
when it comes to the major rules.

The Vinaya lists three different levels of offence. The most
serious offences are the four *parajika,* a word that literally means
defeat:

1. Should any bhikkhu—participating in the training and
   livelihood of the bhikkhus, without having renounced the
   training, without having declared his weakness—engage
   in the sexual act, even with a female animal, he is defeated
   and no longer in communion.
2. Should any bhikkhu, in the manner of stealing, take what
   is not given from an inhabited area or from the wilderness—just as when, in the taking of what is not given, kings
   arresting the criminal would flog, imprison, or banish him,

saying, "You are a robber, you are a fool, you are benighted, you are a thief"—a bhikkhu in the same way taking what is not given is defeated and no longer in communion.

3. Should any bhikkhu intentionally deprive a human being of life, or search for an assassin for him, or praise the advantages of death, or incite him to die (thus): "My good man, what use is this wretched, miserable life to you? Death would be better for you than life," or with such an idea in mind, such a purpose in mind, should in various ways praise the advantages of death or incite him to die, he also is defeated and no longer in communion.

4. Should any bhikkhu, without direct knowledge, boast of a superior human state, a truly noble knowledge and vision as present in himself, saying, "Thus do I know; thus do I see," such that regardless of whether or not he is cross-examined on a later occasion, he —being remorseful and desirous of purification—might say, "Friends, not knowing, I said I know; not seeing, I said I see—vainly, falsely, idly," unless it was from overestimation, he also is defeated and no longer in communion.[3]

These four parajika—sexual intercourse, stealing, killing or abetting the killing of a human being, and falsely claiming spiritual enlightenment—are sometimes called "expulsion offences," but technically that is incorrect because the bhikkhu is not expelled after committing one of these four offences; he simply ceases to be a bhikkhu in the very act of committing it. Zen Master Thich Nhat Hanh, in his updating of the Pratimoksha for the twenty-first century, translates the term as a "Degradation Offence." If a monk breaks any of the Four Degradation Offences, he is "no longer worthy to remain a Bhikshu and cannot participate in the activities of the Bhikshu Sangha."[4]

Each rule is prefaced by a story of a bhikkhu who has transgressed. In the case of sexual intercourse the introductory story concerns an observant bhikkhu whose family was upset with him because he was not providing for an heir. To appease them, he decided that he would engage in a single act of sexual intercourse with his former wife in order to impregnate her. The Vinaya then proceeds to define sexual intercourse: "Whenever the male organ is made to enter the female, even for the length of the fruit of a sesame plant."

As other cases arise—and there are many—the definition of sexual intercourse is expanded and refined: "Any penetration by the male organ into any of the three orifices (mouth, vagina, anus) of any being (male or female, animal or human), or certain classes of supernatural beings, or dead bodies." Any bhikkhu who willingly engages in sexual intercourse of any kind, and does so while conscious, automatically and permanently loses bhikkhu status.

The Vinaya also contains two levels of rules governing sexual activity short of intercourse. At the second level of offence are the *sanghadisesas* (meeting of the sangha). These transgressions demand that the whole monastic community come together to impose on the offending monk the penalty determined by the Buddha for such an infraction. The offending bhikkhu is required to sit, stand, and walk in file in the lowest rank and to confess his offence before the whole community for six consecutive days. If a visiting bhikkhu arrives during his time of public penance, the bhikkhu who has offended must seek him out and tell him what he has done. In any Buddhist country laypeople who frequent a monastery would immediately be aware that a member of the community had committed a sanghadisesa offence because they would see him relegated to the lowest place in the sangha. Since seniority is such an important matter in Buddhist monastic etiquette, this kind of public shaming is an especially severe form of punishment.

There are thirteen sanghadisesas or second-level offences; five of them relate to sexuality.

1. Intentional discharge of semen, except while dreaming, entails initial and subsequent meetings of the Community.
2. Should any bhikkhu, overcome by lust, with altered mind, engage in bodily contact with a woman, or in holding her hand, holding a lock of her hair, or caressing any of her

limbs, it entails initial and subsequent meetings of the Community.

3. Should any bhikkhu, overcome by lust, with altered mind, address lewd words to a woman in the manner of young men to a young woman alluding to sexual intercourse, it entails initial and subsequent meetings of the Community.

4. Should any bhikkhu, overcome by lust, with altered mind, speak in the presence of a woman in praise of ministering to his own sensuality thus: "This, sister, is the highest ministration, that of ministering to a virtuous, fine-natured follower of the celibate life such as myself with this act"—alluding to sexual intercourse—it entails initial and subsequent meetings of the Community.

5. Should any bhikkhu engage in conveying a man's intentions to a woman or a woman's intentions to a man, proposing marriage or paramourage—even if only for a momentary liaison—it entails initial and subsequent meetings of the Community.[5]

The first rule of this second category of offences refers to masturbation, intentionally arousing oneself to the point of ejaculation. A nocturnal emission that occurs during a dream, and is therefore not intentional, is not a sanghadisesa.

Intention is also paramount in the rule outlawing bodily contact with a woman. For this reason, there is no fault if contact is made accidentally or without agreeing to it. However, since it is very difficult for someone to know the intention of another person—indeed, it is difficult to be fully cognizant of one's own intentions—bhikkhus are strongly counseled to avoid any physical contact whatsoever with a woman.

The rule forbidding speaking lewd words to a woman "in the manner of young men to a young woman," is precisely defined in the Vinaya text as any words spoken for the purpose of teasing or titillation, and any mention of the female sexual organs, the anus, or sexual intercourse. Lewd remarks other than these are considered a lesser offence.

The rule prohibiting bhikkhus from facilitating the sexual activity of laypeople obviously applies to a bhikkhu who would act as a pimp as well as to a bhikkhu who would make arrangements for people to have sex. But this offence would also be committed by a bhikkhu who officiated at a marriage ceremony. For this reason, some bhikkhus, when asked to perform a wedding will jokingly respond that they only perform happy ceremonies—like funerals. It should be noted, however, that the Vinaya does not prohibit a bhikkhu from blessing a couple after they are formally married or helping a separated couple become reconciled.

As has been pointed out, a parajika offence automatically results in permanent separation from the sangha since it is seen as evidence that the offender has a mind incapable of enlightenment, which is the whole reason for the monastic order and the monastic pursuit. A sanghadisesa offence shows that one has clearly lost the way, but that there is still a chance for rehabilitation.

Finally, the Vinaya includes several minor offences that are cleared simply by confession to another bhikkhu. Those having to do with sexuality most often concern being alone with a woman and contact between bhikkhus and bhikkhunis. For example:

- Should any bhikkhu lie down in the same lodging with a woman, it is to be confessed.
- Should any bhikkhu teach more than five or six sentences of Dhamma to a woman, unless a knowledgeable man is present, it is to be confessed.
- Should any bhikkhu, unauthorized, exhort the bhikkhunis, it is to be confessed.
- Should any bhikkhu, even if authorized, exhort the bhikkhunis after sunset, it is to be confessed.
- Should any bhikkhu, having gone to the bhikkhunis' quarters, exhort the bhikkhunis—except at the proper occasion—it is to be confessed. Here the proper occasion is this: A bhikkhuni is ill. This is the proper occasion here.[6]

Even though no sexual conversation or activity takes place, the very fact that a bhikkhu is alone with women is grounds for a fault. For this reason, a bhikkhu who visits laypeople is usually accompanied by another bhikkhu or a male attendant.

Part of the reason for the regulations of the Vinaya regarding the sexual behavior of bhikkhus is the concern to avoid even the appearance of impropriety. Bhikkhus do not work at occupations that generate salaries, and therefore the sangha relies entirely on the support of the lay community. For this reason it is of utmost importance that bhikkhus earn the respect of the laity by maintaining the highest standards of conduct and by devoting themselves wholeheartedly to their spiritual practice.

While some rules might seem excessively strict or prudish, their good sense quickly becomes apparent in the wake of a scandal caused by a bhikkhu's misconduct, or in the event of a rumor that began when someone observed a bhikkhu in a situation that could suggest dalliance. Sexual misconduct of any kind—even the appearance of sexual misbehavior—is especially destructive of the laity's regard for a monastic community and, of course, of the integrity of the community itself. For this reason, the Vinaya insists on the greatest measure of discretion in order to avoid any occasion that could lead a bhikkhu astray or be misinterpreted by someone who happened upon a bhikkhu in a situation that laid him open to suspicion.

The avoidance of scandal, however, is not the principal reason the Vinaya prohibits bhikkhus and bhikkhunis from engaging in any and all sexual activity. According to the teaching of the Buddha, "There is no fire like lust, there is no evil like anger and hatred, there is no ill like the burden of the five aggregates of existence and there is no bliss like the Perfect Peace of Nibbana."[7]

The story connected with this particular verse of the Dhammapada describes an occasion when the Buddha and his bhikkhus were invited to a wedding celebration. The bridegroom had become so sexually aroused by the sight of his bride that he neglected the duties of hospitality. To remove his emotional attachment for the time being and to divert his attention, the Buddha willed that the bride become invisible to the bridegroom and thus not distract him from giving his guests the attention they deserved. When the Buddha spoke his word, both bride and bridegroom realized the Dhamma. "At that moment, the Buddha permitted them to see each other once more, but there was no longer any passionate excitement between them, for they had realized the true nature of worldly experience."[8]

The point of the story, and of the teaching it contains, is that there is no sensual pleasure that creates attachment as strong as that created by sexual stimulation. It, more than any other attachment, keeps one from enlightenment. At the same time, once one has realized the true nature of worldly experience, namely, that it ultimately leads to dukkha, one is free of the attachment to sensual pleasure that sexual stimulation normally brings about.

Another verse of the Dhammapada emphasizes that lust inevitably leads to pain and sorrow. The story here is of a young man whose fiancée became ill and died on the way to the wedding. The Buddha, knowing that the time was ripe for the bridegroom to realize the Dhamma, went to visit him. After hearing the story of the tragic death of his fiancée, the Buddha said, "Lust begets sorrow; it is due to lust for things and lust for sensual pleasures that sorrow and fear arise." Again the teaching for monks would be clear: to the degree that you avoid lusting after sensual pleasures, you will be free of sorrow and fear, you will realize the purpose for which you have chosen the way of celibacy.

Unlike the Buddhist Pratimoksha, with its detailed rules for avoiding sexual misconduct and for responding to sexual transgressions, the Rule of Benedict contains no specific rules that address the sexual conduct of the monk. The omission of such guidelines is a departure from a monastic tradition that goes back to Pachomius, the fourth-century Egyptian founder of cenobitic monasticism, whose *Precepts* are very specific about the kinds of behavior that monks are to avoid so as not to be a source of temptation to one another. They should, for example, cover their knees when sitting;[9] not do the laundry with their clothes drawn up higher than is established; not sit two together on a mat or a carpet; not sit together on a barebacked donkey; not speak to another in the place where they sleep.[10]

Benedict's references to sexual behavior are much more general, implicit, and, shall we say, "spiritual." The Rule's chapter on "The Instruments of Good Works" (4) includes the biblical commandment "not to commit adultery." It also urges monks "to love chastity" and "not to fulfill the desires of the flesh." The chapter also includes a very Buddhist-sounding admonition "not to become attached to pleasures." The abbot is to be "chaste, sober, and merciful" (64). The penultimate chapter of the Rule, "On the Good Zeal Which Monks Are to Have" (72), counsels the monks to "tender the charity of brotherhood chastely, fear God in love, love their Abbot with a sincere and humble charity."

In chapter 22, "How the Monks Are to Sleep," it may be possible to detect Benedict's concern to remove—or at least to mitigate—conditions that could lead a brother to temptation and transgression. In the very first sentence of this chapter Benedict stipulates that each monk is to sleep in his own bed. If possible, he wants one common dormitory and prescribes that a candle be kept burning in the room until morning. The younger brethren are not to have beds next to one another, but among those of the older ones.

Benedict also wants his monks to sleep in their monastic habits, though the reason he gives for this regulation is that the monks not dawdle when getting up for the night Office. They are to be "always ready to rise without delay when the signal is given and hasten to be before one another at the Work of God." That there be no tarrying on the way to Vigils is also the principal reason given in the Rule of the Master, the monastic rule from which much of the Rule of Benedict is derived. The Rule of the Master does add, however, that "The brethren are to sleep clothed and girded so that a brother may not touch his naked members. For thereby lustful impurities are brought into the soul."[11] In the same chapter, the Rule of the Master also makes it clear that the reason the deans (i.e., monks in charge of a "deanery," that is, a group of ten monks) are to have beds near the brothers is "so that during the night they may correct any vicious faults of theirs."

Benedict's provision that baths "be afforded the sick as often as may be expedient; but to the healthy, and especially to the young, let them be granted more rarely" (ch. 36) may have something to do with his desire to reduce occasions that could give rise to sexual temptation. However, the impression one gets from this passage is that his primary objective is to remove from the monastery all forms of a lifestyle that could be considered luxurious.

As many have pointed out, what characterizes the Rule of Benedict is its insistence that "all things be done with moderation" (48:9). The Rule's virtual silence regarding sexuality may be an indication of Benedict's rejection of the fixation on sexual temptations that marked the lives of some early monks and the extreme measures they took to repress their sexual thoughts and desires. While it is true that the struggle of the monks who fled to the desert wilderness was directed primarily against anger and spiritual sloth, and that lust as a secondary vice was given much less consideration,[12] the literature that came from this early period of the monastic movement contains vivid, even shocking, stories about monks like Ammonius, who seared his flesh with a red-hot iron; or Pachon, who put an asp next to his genitals; or Evagrius, who cooled his passion for a noblewoman by submerging himself in an icy well.[13] While the genre of these stories may be more like tabloid journalism than accurate reporting, they did distort the way Christians in general, and monks in particular, thought about sexuality.

Another possible explanation for Benedict's seeming reluctance to provide a lot of specific rules regarding the sexual behavior of monks is that this matter was given such extensive and, for that time, at least, balanced treatment by John Cassian, whose *Conferences* and *Institutes* are explicitly commended in the Rule. In chapter 42, "That No One Speak after Compline," the *Conferences* are listed among the works that are to be read to the brothers during the time between the evening meal and the praying of Compline. The Rule ends with this encomium to the works of Cassian and to other monastic teachings: "Then the Conferences and the Institutes and the Lives of the Fathers, as also the Rule of our holy Father Basil—what else are they but tools of virtue for right-living and obedient monks?" (ch. 73).[14]

John Cassian (ca. 360–433) was one of the most prolific of early Christian monastic authors. His twenty-four *Conferences* and twelve *Institutes* constitute about twelve hundred pages of printed material and recount the lives and teachings of the fourth-century monks of the Egyptian desert. Cassian had visited these monastic communities after having spent some time living as a monk in a hermitage near Bethlehem. The spiritual teachings and examples of virtuous living he received during that journey and subsequently committed to writing had a profound impact on the development of Western monasticism. The sixth *Institute*, "The Spirit of Fornication," and the twelfth and twenty-second *Conferences*, "On Chastity" and "The Illusions of the Night"—that is, orgasmic dreams—are devoted to the subject of chastity. In Cassian's *opus* only prayer receives more attention. How to channel one's sexual energy was obviously a topic of intense interest for those early Christian monks, as it continues to be today.

The relatively large amount of attention Cassian gives to the matter of sexuality in his writings on the monastic life may seem excessive, but Cassian was no fanatic. His approach to the topic is calm and objective. At the same time, because of the particular sexual issues he addresses, his teaching on chastity can appear a bit wacky to the contemporary reader, especially his extended treatment of nocturnal emissions as a spiritual problem. In an age when the harm done by the sexual wrongdoing of some clergy and religious has so shaken the church and the public, giving attention to wet dreams can seem quaint, even ludicrous.

Cassian's frankness about sexual functions was by no means typical of Christian spiritual writers. Indeed, it was so shocking to the nineteenth-century translators of his works that they left these three treatises in Latin. Nowadays we pride ourselves on our candor about sexuality, but when a classical spiritual writer starts analyzing the causes of penile erection, even a modern-day reader still squirms a bit. Does he have to be so graphic?

The reason Cassian speaks so directly and concretely about nocturnal emission is that his whole take on chastity revolves around a careful analysis of what is in our minds, and therefore in our dreams and in our bodies. His position is that if in sleep we regularly experience erotic fantasies that lead to emission, we are not yet chaste. Through constant vigilance a monk may succeed in being continent, but continence is not chastity. A monk to whom God grants the gift of chastity may have the occasional nocturnal emission, but it will not be accompanied by erotic dreams. As long as one's dream life includes sexual fantasies, chastity remains unrealized. On the other hand, if a monk is untroubled by sexual thoughts and fantasies when he is sleeping, that is to say, even when he is not able to be vigilant, that is the ultimate confirmation of the presence of chastity.

The distinction between continence and chastity is crucial for Cassian. By continence he means conscious, ascetic control of one's sexual impulse. That kind of control is fine and good and is to be striven for, but it is not yet chastity. In Columba Stewart's words, "Ascetical discipline can battle lust to a truce, but only grace can bring freedom."[15] The Christian virtue of chastity goes beyond continence in that moral control has been internalized. A chaste person no longer has to resist temptation in order to avoid sexual transgressions. He experiences freedom from physical arousal, sexual fantasies, and their incentive to sinful behavior. To use a musical image: continence is practicing the scales and memorizing the notes; chastity is making incredibly beautiful music, and doing so in a way that appears and feels effortless. Or, to use an analogy that would be immediately intelligible to anyone familiar with the world of Alcoholics Anonymous, continence is a dry drunk; chastity is sobriety.

Cassian's understanding of chastity may seem hopelessly idealistic to people—monks included—in the twenty-first century. To tell the truth, some of his contemporaries felt the same way. Cassian's response to them was that they should not dismiss his teaching as impossible before they had actually tried it. He himself, he said, had put it into practice and it worked. He admitted that the level of chastity he attained might not have

been as high as that of the holiest of the monks, but it nevertheless went beyond mere continence; it was characterized by joy
in purity.

Cassian's position is that once you arrive at chastity, you will
find that you no longer have frequent sexual dreams and emissions. To the objection that these bodily movements are produced
by the unconscious and therefore beyond our control, Cassian
responded that they nevertheless depend very much on how we
use our conscious hours. If a monk, rather than filling his heart
with wholesome thoughts during his waking hours, entertains
lascivious fantasies, he can hardly hope to be free of dreams that
stimulate him sexually. This point of view is made explicit in the
Rule of the Master. In a chapter entitled "Whether Brothers who
have Suffered Pollution during Sleep Should Receive Communion or Not," it says of monks who frequently have wet dreams,
"let them know that it is not by accident but by their own choice
that they are incurring excommunication. They are the ones es-
tranging themselves from the body of God because by their
thoughts they feed their own lust and are responsible for defiling
their body through impure desires" (ch. LXXX).

Modern psychology would object that our dream life is not
what Cassian thinks it is. Unconscious hours are a time for com-
pensation, the period when our various drives and frustrations
get worked out. Not only are we not responsible for what happens in sleep, dreams need to happen in order to relieve us of
unbearable stresses and strains. To hope for a time when we will
be without erotic dreams is to live in fairy-tale land.

Cassian, of course, did not know about Freud and therefore
he never heard of the unconscious. It is possible that he would
have regarded it as a useful category, but he probably would
resist thinking of it as a hermetically sealed compartment. One
of his constant emphases is the interconnectedness of the person. For him, the waking and the sleeping hours are intimately
linked, and so are all the facets of the person: body, soul, and
spirit. That is the reason his discussions of chastity range widely
over the whole field of the virtues. One of the corollaries of his
holistic approach to chastity is that he considers it a key to the

whole spiritual and moral life. He believes that one's sexual life is a good barometer of one's overall spiritual health. For Cassian the absence of erotic dreams is the final stage in one's progress toward perfect chastity and perfect love, which is the goal of the Christian life.

Even though the Vinaya explicitly excludes the unintentional emission of semen from the list of sanghadisesa offences, the teaching of Cassian on the cause of erotic dreams resonates strongly with the Buddhist emphasis on the importance of attending to the conscious mind. What we do with our conscious mind during the day really determines what happens to us during the night; how we live our lives daily affects our dream life.

Cassian's integralist approach enables him to craft a subtle, indirect morality of chastity. He often writes about the relation of chastity to the other moral virtues, and he continually points out that there is no way to achieve chastity without developing the other virtues. Thus, without gentleness, patience, and especially humility, it is useless to hope for chastity. This linkage to the other virtues highlights the "social" dimension of the virtue of chastity. Stewart observes that "With the growth of chastity comes the possibility of human relationships founded truly on love rather than selfish desire or vainglorious manipulation."[16]

At the same time, Cassian teaches that chastity is unlike the other virtues in that it cannot be promoted by interaction with other people. He claims that one must flee others because others tempt us to unchastity. For that reason he does not think that the monk who lives in community can achieve chastity; all that is possible for him is continence. There is some ambiguity, however, in Cassian's teaching. Stewart notes that some of Cassian's harshest words are reserved for false anchorites who simply do not want to deal with other people. And Cassian himself, both in theory and in practice, placed high value on friendship.[17]

Many, of course, would disagree with Cassian's position that community is a hindrance to chastity, pointing out that solitude undertaken as an escape or at too early a stage in one's spiritual life can be the worst milieu for chastity. Thomas Merton, for example, in one of his conferences to the novices at Gethsemani, said about this teaching of Cassian that some souls in solitude find that their imagination runs riot, and are better under control in a social life where there is some activity to keep them occupied.[18]

Cassian's stress on life experience and practice shows that he is not simply an idealist about chastity. He provides a concrete program of ascetic preparation for chastity. When he and his fellow monk and friend Germanus went on their tour of Egyptian monasteries, one of the monks they visited pointed out that wandering around Egypt and collecting the wisdom of the elders was worthless if one did not submit oneself to an ascetical program. In order to arrive at perfect chastity, it is necessary that one's program include the following:

1. Refraining from idle gossip;
2. Abstaining from all anger and worldly care;
3. Being content with only two dried loaves of bread (*paxamatia*) a day;
4. Not drinking your fill of water;
5. Sleeping only three to four hours;
6. Believing that chastity is only attained by the mercy of God.[19]

After following such a regimen for six months Cassian believed a person would know "if such perfection is not impossible for him." In other words, devoting a half year to these ascetical practices will not necessarily make one chaste, but it will allow one to determine whether or not chastity is a real possibility. "Cassian is providing a tool to discern entry into a process," comments Stewart, "not a plan for crossing the finish line."[20]

In spite of Cassian's final admonition to trust in God's mercy, some have seen in these directives an indication that his teaching, especially as put forward in the thirteenth Conference, "On Divine Protection," attributes a life of true virtue to the vigorous exercise of free will rather than to the grace of God. In fact, after his death Cassian was accused of the heresy known as semi-Pelagianism, which taught that the process of salvation begins with an individual's free choice and is then perfected and com-

pleted by divine grace, rather than being, in its entirely, beginning to end, the free gift of God.

Semi-Pelagianism was condemned by the Second Council
of Orange, and because the council's decrees were seen as a
vindication of the teaching of Augustine, with whom Cassian
disagreed on some points, its anathema cast a cloud over Cassian. As a result he was never officially recognized as a saint by
the Catholic Church. It is interesting to note, however, that the
Council of Orange took place in 529, the year traditionally given
for the composition of the Rule of Benedict, the last chapter of
which extols Cassian as a teacher whose works are to be read
and followed because they are "tools of virtue for right-living
and obedient monks" (ch. 73).

A careful reading of Cassian's teaching on chastity makes it
clear that he regards God's grace as absolutely essential for the
spiritual progress of the monk, and specifically for arriving at
perfect chastity. While he emphasizes that ascetical practices are
necessary, he recognizes that they do not lead to chastity directly. In fact, these ascetical practices, like the Jewish Law according to Saint Paul's teaching, actually serve to bring us face
to face with our sin.[21] According to one Cassian scholar, ascetical
practices produce the knowledge that chastity is not attained by
such efforts and the recognition that one must humbly rely on
the grace of God.[22] Until the monk is really perfect, long periods
of abstinence will make him think that his chastity is his own
doing. When that happens, God abandons him for his own
good. In thought or deed he offends against chastity and, by the
grace of God, returns again to the one who alone can give the
grace of perfect chastity.

Cassian was well aware that he was proposing an ideal of
human sexual purity that is well beyond human capability. Of
course, one must strive to be chaste, because without constant
effort and watchfulness on our part, lust will win out. But Cassian insisted again and again that the virtue of chastity is a gift
of God and not a reward for human striving.

The battle against the spirit of fornication is the second
battle, following that against gluttony, but it will not be totally

overcome until all the other vices are uprooted. The setbacks the monk will inevitably experience in the battle against the spirit of fornication will keep him humble and teach him that it is God who enables him to overcome all vices and progress in virtue.[23] For this reason Cassian holds that the spiritual disciplines of reading, meditation, and unceasing prayer are more important than physical disciplines. They fill the mind and heart with good thoughts and keep the monk constantly aware of a loving and powerful God, who alone can grant the freedom, peace, and tranquility of perfect chastity.

Cassian sees sexuality in general and sexual dreams in particular as a touchstone, a measuring device to determine the state of the monk's heart. As long as a monk is still attached to things, and especially to sensual pleasure, he has not yet arrived at that blessed purity of heart that will allow him to see God.[24] At the same time, a monk's failure to be chaste, his giving in to sexual fantasies and actions, can actually bring about the humility to trust more deeply in the God he is seeking.

Chapter 5

Stumbling on the Path
Repentance and Reintegration
or Expulsion?

Sexuality is not only the most intense, but also the most am-
biguous and unpredictable of all our impulses. Just when someone thinks he has succeeding in quieting the shrill insistence of
hyperactive hormones and being able simply to observe and let
go of fantasies that promise everlasting bliss with the partner of
his dreams, he can be overtaken by a passion so strong that he
is willing to risk reputation, fortune, and family in order to satisfy it. Thomas Merton, as we have seen, struggled to remain
faithful to his love for the monastic life while falling in love with
an attractive and sensitive nurse who cared for him. His account
of how sexual attraction consumed his life echoes the experience
of real and fictitious couples such as David and Bathsheba,
Tristan and Isolde, Anthony and Cleopatra, Abelard and Heloise, Romeo and Juliet, Anna Karenina and Vronsky, who have
become icons of romantic love in Western literature. The main
difference, of course, is that Merton was able to turn back from
a path that he knew could not possibly lead to their living "happily ever after" and might well ruin their lives.

The Buddha and his disciples reflect a universal human experience when they single out sex as the king of desires. While
it may be true that faced with death by starvation, we would
willingly and without a moment's hesitation sacrifice sexual
pleasure for a piece of bread, it is also obvious that lust can
provoke behavior that any clear-headed person would reject as

stupid, bizarre, or insane. The expression "madly in love" is actually quite accurate. Scientific studies have shown that the brain chemistry of people who are infatuated is similar to that of people with mental illness. A report on the research of anthropologist Helen Fisher describes how love lights up the caudate nucleus because it is home to a dense spread of receptors for a neurotransmitter called dopamine, part of our own "endogenous love potion." In the right proportions, dopamine creates intense energy, exhilaration, focused attention, and motivation to win rewards. It leads us to ignore social conventions, even deeply held ethical and religious convictions, and to take risks that we would never dream of taking in our more level-headed moments.[1]

At the same time, a love affair so passionate and all-consuming that life is inconceivable without it can turn into intense revulsion or fade away into oblivion. In Alan Renais's groundbreaking film *Hiroshima mon Amour* (1959) a French actress has an adulterous tryst with a Japanese architect while in Hiroshima for the shooting of a film. She tells him about her love affair with a German soldier in Nevers during the Second World War and of his death at the hands of the resistance on the very day they were to leave together for Bavaria. The passion of that ill-fated liaison was beyond anything she had ever experienced before or after. But having first forgotten his eyes, and then the sound of his voice, she confesses that she can no longer even remember what he looked like.

While the primary myth about sexuality, at least in contemporary American culture, is that it is an urge so basic and strong that we risk doing grave harm to our emotional and even physical well-being if we do not satisfy it, a contradictory myth is also in force. That myth holds that those who have opted for celibacy—all the more, those who have taken a vow of chastity—are thereby capable of exercising complete control over all their sexual impulses. When it comes to celibacy, there is no room for growth. A celibate life has to be lived perfectly *ab initio*. Any failure to preserve "perfect chastity" is immediately interpreted as proof of hypocrisy, turpitude, or a shameful lack of self-control.[2]

Common sense, however, would lead one to expect that even those who are sincere in their desire to live chastely and celibately in order to devote themselves to the monastic way of life will at times fail, and may even fail seriously. Sometimes pride is the reason: I am so spiritually mature that I couldn't possibly get into trouble. Sometimes carelessness or naiveté: It just never occurred to me that there would be any problem if we slept in the same bed. Sometimes disappointment, setback, or ennui—the classical Christian monastic term is *acedia* or "the noonday devil"—intensifies the feelings of isolation and loneliness to such an extent that one becomes desperate for companionship and physical intimacy. Lacking the guidance of a spiritual mentor or the support of one's brothers, the danger of initiating a sexual relationship with another person—maybe even a brother monk—becomes all the greater.

Sometimes such a relationship is entered into with full awareness of how "unskillful" it will prove to be, sometimes with the adolescent rationalization that if "it feels so right, it can't possibly be wrong," sometimes with the more "adult" rationalization of entitlement: I've given up so much; I'm entitled to a little reprieve. It is even possible for a monk to convince himself that engaging in a sexually intimate relationship will actually help him become a more compassionate, more sensitive, even a more spiritual human being. The reason I am so withdrawn, so unfeeling, he rationalizes, is because I have never "really" loved. Platonic love won't do it; I need to become physically intimate with someone. Then I will become whole.

Sometimes a monk can simply become lax and neglect the daily practices that keep him faithful to the commitments he has made. And sometimes, especially if he has had little or no experience with romantic relationships, he can be seduced. But even though a monk has failed to keep his vow of celibate chastity by having intercourse, a Catholic response to such failure allows for the possibility of repentance, conversion, and indeed a more mature commitment to a celibate way of life.

Saint Benedict's Rule for monasteries, unlike the Vinaya, does not classify sexual intercourse as an offence that automatically excludes one from the monastic life. In fact, as has already been noted, the Rule makes no explicit reference to sexual misconduct.[3] Benedict does elaborate an extensive penal code to deal with monks who are "obstinate, or disobedient, or proud, or murmuring, or habitually transgress the Holy Rule in any point" (ch. 23), and in it he lays out a series of responses to transgressions that become increasingly severe: private admonition, public rebuke, excommunication from the common table and prayer, and finally corporal punishment.[4] But nowhere in the Rule are these penalties explicitly directed to a monk who has engaged in sexual activity, whether alone or with others.

The disciplinary measures outlined by Benedict undoubtedly made more sense in a society that placed great value on participation in community activities and took corporal punishment for granted. In today's Western society, at least, with its stress on individuality and free choice, and in which being "grounded" is the ultimate form of punishment for a teenager, excommunicating a monk from the common table and community prayer would usually not be experienced as any great hardship.

While the provisions of the penal code may appear severe by modern standards, it must be pointed out that what is especially emphasized in this section of the Rule is how solicitous the abbot must be for those undergoing discipline. He is to remember Jesus' teaching that it is not the healthy, but the sick, who need a physician. He is to provide the offending monk with *sympectae*, "brethren of mature years and wisdom," to counsel and console him that he may not be overcome by excessive grief (RB, ch. 27).

Moreover, the disciplines imposed are described not so much as punishment but as a way of helping the offending monk recognize his failure and return to the path he had abandoned. Still, Benedict does recognize that there will be monks who refuse to amend their lives, and for them the only response is to use "the knife of amputation . . . lest one diseased sheep contaminate the whole flock" (RB, ch. 28).

In the Rule of Benedict there is no such thing as automatic expulsion from the community for particular offences. Benedict lets the abbot determine when it may be necessary to expel a disobedient and recalcitrant monk who refuses to change his ways. Universal church law, on the other hand, has identified two transgressions that constitute an *ipso facto* or automatic expulsion from monastic and other forms of vowed religious life—transgressions that function, in other words, like a parajika. According to Canon 694 of the Code of Canon Law, "A member must be held as *ipso facto* dismissed from an institute who has defected notoriously from the Catholic faith [or who] has contracted marriage or attempted it, even only civilly." Sexual intercourse of itself does not result in automatic dismissal.

A Catholic monk who engages in sexual intercourse clearly violates his vow of chastity in addition to committing a serious sin against the sixth commandment. One who commits such an offence is required to confess it to a priest, receive sacramental absolution, carry out the prescribed penance, and avoid those situations that could cause him to fall again. He may also have certain restrictions placed on his activities and could be removed from certain forms of pastoral ministry. Repeated failures to live celibately would be grounds for dismissal from a monastic or other religious community, but the process is long and complicated, owing to the fact that universal church law is weighted to safeguard the rights of the individual. On the other hand, if the offender repents and makes a sincere and serious effort to reform his life, he will be forgiven and allowed to continue in the brotherhood. If his superior, after having taken counsel, judges that there is no risk of recidivism, he may also be allowed to engage in ministerial activities once again.

In recent years, as the general public has become increasingly aware of the harm that can result from the immoral sexual behavior of a person who is in a position of authority, especially when that authority is spiritual, there has been a growing recognition of the need to take into account the damage that can be done to people who have been enticed or coerced into a sexual relationship by a priest or vowed religious. Monastic and other religious communities have also come to recognize that they have a responsibility to help victims recover from the emotional

and spiritual harm they have suffered, as well as to guide offenders to sincere repentance of the wrong they have done and
to the reformation of their lives.

The instances of sexual abuse by American Catholic priests
and religious that came to light during recent decades brought
about a much clearer awareness of the particularly damaging
consequences of sexual abuse on minors. In response to the
scandal of clergymen and religious who had sexually abused
children and adolescents, the United States bishops decided that
any Catholic priest or deacon guilty of this kind of sexual abuse
would automatically be barred from all acts of public ministry.
This decision was promulgated in a 2002 document entitled *Essential Norms*, which was then reissued with Vatican approval in
2006.[5] Paragraph eight of their document reads as follows:

> When even a single act of sexual abuse by a priest or deacon
> is admitted or is established after an appropriate process in
> accord with canon law, the offending priest or deacon will be
> removed permanently from ecclesiastical ministry, not exclud-
> ing dismissal from the clerical state, if the case so warrants.

This section of the *Essential Norms* thus became "particular
law" for the United States, making specific the nature of the
"just penalties" referred to in Canon 1395 of the Code of Canon
Law:

> A cleric who in another way has committed an offense against
> the sixth commandment of the Decalogue, if the delict was
> committed by force or threats or publicly or with a minor
> below the age of sixteen years is to be punished with just pen-
> alties, not excluding dismissal from the clerical state if the case
> so warrants.[6]

In a certain sense the "one strike and you're out" response
of the United States Conference of Catholic Bishops to a priest
who had sexually abused a minor is similar to the Vinaya's clas-
sification of sexual intercourse as a parajika. There is a significant difference, however, in that the U.S. bishops decided to

include virtually all serious sexual offences, and not just intercourse, as grounds for removing a priest from ecclesiastical ministry, and possibly from the clerical state.

According to the *Essential Norms*, sexual abuse of a minor includes sexual molestation or sexual exploitation of a minor and other behavior by which an adult uses a minor as an object of sexual gratification. In assessing an allegation of sexual abuse of a minor, what is to be determined is not whether or not the conduct or interaction fell within the civil definitions of abuse, but whether the behavior qualified as an external, objectively grave violation of the sixth commandment, which, in Catholic theology, has traditionally been interpreted as a prohibition of all sexual activity outside of marriage. The *Essential Norms* specifically state that a canonical offence against the sixth commandment of the Decalogue need not be a complete act of intercourse. Nor, to be objectively grave, does an act need to involve force, physical contact, or a discernible harmful outcome.

The note to this paragraph suggests that there is some latitude when it comes to determining the seriousness of a particular offence against the sixth commandment:

> If there is any doubt whether a specific act qualifies as an external, objectively grave violation, the writings of recognized moral theologians should be consulted, and the opinions of recognized experts should be appropriately obtained. Ultimately, it is the responsibility of the diocesan bishop/eparch, with the advice of a qualified review board, to determine the gravity of the alleged act.[7]

The American bishops made it clear that the *Essential Norms* put forth to respond to cases of clerical sexual abuse of minors also applied to "clerical religious institutes, and societies of apostolic life of the United States with respect to all priests and deacons in the ecclesiastical ministry of the Church in the United States." But they also recognized that a major superior of a clerical religious institute—for example, an abbot of a monastic community— or society of apostolic life could apply and interpret them for the internal life and governance of the institute or society, provided he did so according to the universal law of the church and the proper law of the institute or society.[8]

The religious (including monastic) superiors of the United States, through their official organization, the Conference of Major Superiors of Men (CMSM), determined that members of their communities who had sexually abused children or adolescents would not normally be expelled from their communities. In a statement entitled "Improving Pastoral Care and Accountability in Response to the Tragedy of Sexual Abuse,"[9] issued at their annual assembly in August 2002, they explained that because their religious vows bound them together in community, they were called to respond compassionately to any of their members who had committed this violence against a young person. They continued to regard them as their brothers in Christ and shared their burden. In spite of their sins, those who had offended remained part of their family, and for this reason they could not turn their backs on their brothers.

They agreed, however, that if a religious had abused a child or adolescent, he was not only subject to civil and criminal law, but, according to the *Charter for the Protection of Children and Young People*, he also could not be reassigned to public ministries or be involved with young people. Though it might be long in coming, they would walk the journey with him through repentance, healing, forgiveness, and hopefully reconciliation.

The members of CMSM went on to say that compassion did not cloud their clarity. They abhorred sexual abuse and would not tolerate any type of abuse by their members. Drawing on their tradition of fraternal correction, they would hold one another accountable. Since, in addition to being a crime, the sexual abuse of minors violated the most fundamental values held by religious, members who had offended would be placed under severe restrictions after treatment, and those who posed the greatest danger to the public would be carefully supervised to avoid any situation in which they might engage in abuse again.

As part of their response to the sexual abuse crisis, religious orders determined to formulate and adopt specific rules and guidelines to help celibate men recognize and avoid situations that could lead to sexual misconduct, as well as to respond to victims and perpetrators when transgressions occurred.

Rules and regulations, of course, are no guarantee that a monk will sustain a chaste celibate life. In the case of Catholic monks, if the intention to follow Christ in chaste celibacy is lacking—an intention that must be bolstered by prayer, meditation, good counsel, and the support of peers if it is to be translated into the way one actually lives one's life—almost any rule or regulation can be ignored or rationalized away on the grounds that "it doesn't apply to me in this particular case."

Nonetheless, the experience of both Buddhist and Christian monastic communities over the centuries has shown that a desire to live celibately, even when buoyed up by a discipline of spiritual practice and the support of a community, still needs to be shored up by legislation that explicitly prohibits certain kinds of behavior. In the area of sexuality, the possibilities for self-deception are virtually infinite— a situation likely to be as true for people who are married as it is for those who are celibate.

In order to elaborate policies and procedures that reflected the best practices in response to the tragedy of sexual abuse, especially the abuse of minors, the Conference of Major Superiors of Men contracted with Praesidium, Inc., a professional organization that deals in abuse risk management. After extensive consultations between Praesidium and CMSM, a set of policies was forwarded to all religious institutes to guide them in setting up their own policies for preventing sexual misconduct by their members (those who had made vows, as well as novices, and candidates), for responding to victims of abuse, and for supervising offenders.[10] The contract with Praesidium also included an agreement that each participating religious institute would undergo an accrediting visitation to verify that it had policies in place and was following them.

The specific purpose of the policies provided by Praesidium and CMSM is to prevent sexual misconduct between a male religious and any person, adult or minor, to whom he is providing pastoral care, to respond to victims with compassion and justice if an offence does occur, and to ensure that the offending religious is provided appropriate therapy and supervision. The policies also specify the kind of sexual misconduct that, according to the *Essential Norms* of the U.S. bishops, would bar from public ministry a deacon or priest who had even one instance of sexual contact with a minor. Moreover, the policies describe in concrete and specific terms those situations and actions that cause harm and can lead to more serious offences against celibacy and chastity, even if they are entered into or engaged in without any intent to harm another person.

The policies identify prohibited behaviors and define "sexual contact" and "sexual exploitation" with a precision similar to that found in the Vinaya. Sexual contact is "vaginal intercourse, anal intercourse, oral intercourse or the touching of an erogenous zone of another (including but not limited to the thighs, genitals, buttocks, pubic region or chest) for the purpose of sexually arousing or gratifying either person." Sexual exploitation "is sexual contact between a Member and a person with whom the Member has a pastoral relationship. The nature of the relationship is exploitation, regardless of who initiates the sexual contact." The document then goes on to say, "Members must never engage in sexual contact with the persons with whom they have a pastoral relationship. This includes consensual contact, forced physical contact, and sexually explicit conversations not related to counseling issues."

The document becomes extremely specific with regard to minors, defining prohibited behaviors, providing regulations for off-site events, and describing appropriate and inappropriate physical contact. This precision no doubt reflects the greater degree of harm that can be caused when minors are involved. It is probably also a reflection of actual situations that religious superiors have had to deal with.

The standards of conduct for ministry with minors in church-sponsored and affiliated programs prohibit any use or possession of drugs or alcohol, swearing or using foul language, being nude in the presence of minors, sleeping with them, speaking graphically about sexual activities or allowing others to do so,[11] showing them pornographic materials, using one's role in ministry to degrade or humiliate another person. With regard to physical contact, in addition to forbidding such obviously inappropriate gestures as touching a minor's buttocks, chest, or genital area, the standards of conduct ban such behavior as giving piggyback rides, holding minors over two years old on the lap, tickling them, and offering them compliments that relate to physique or body development.

The document includes a section devoted to policies for maintaining ethical ministry with adults and provides a number of specific guidelines. For example, such ministry is not to take place in private living quarters or bedrooms, is to be done with appropriate training or supervision, is to be logged, is to be kept confidential, and must avoid any conflict of interest. There is also a list of "warning signs of boundary violations" such as spending extra time grooming yourself when you know you are going to see a certain person, keeping aspects of your relationship with a person secret from others (such as how often you talk on the phone or see each other alone), giving and receiving special gifts from a certain person, and fantasizing or daydreaming about a certain person.

While it may seem surprising—even shocking to some—that religious institutes would go into such detail about the kinds of behavior to be avoided and boundaries to be observed by adult men who have taken a vow of celibacy, the monastic traditions of both Buddhism and Christianity point to the necessity of such precision. The monastic code of Buddhism came into being because of the necessity to respond to specific complaints about the behavior of bhikkhus. The Catholic monastic tradition also has a long tradition of casuistry—that is to say, developing rules and policies out of actual cases. In the later decades of the twentieth century, however, theological textbooks dealing with ethical issues began to emphasize the essential components of mature and responsible ethical decisions rather than simply listing cases that provided ready-made answers for specific situations. The painful experiences of the last decade, however, have shown how necessary it is to be concrete and specific about inappropriate behavior, especially when trying to keep in check the sexual urges and fantasies that can so easily lead one astray.

Rule and laws of themselves cannot bring about the human and spiritual transformation that is the goal of the monastic life. But they can, especially when interpreted and enforced by an enlightened spiritual mentor, prevent a monk from harming himself and others. If that spiritual mentor is the kind of person Benedict wants the abbot to be: one who exalts mercy above judgment, teaches by word and example, hates vices but loves the brethren, is able to adjust and adapt himself to all, does not go to excess in administering correction, eradicates vices prudently and with charity, taking care that the bruised reed not be broken and remembering that what he has undertaken is the care of weak souls and not a tyranny over strong ones, then it is possible that even a monk who has gravely transgressed may once again return to the monastic path and attain to the loftier heights of doctrine and virtue.[12]

Chapter 6

Persevering on the Path
Facing Challenges Old and New

Those who thought that masturbation was a peculiarly Catholic hang-up may have been surprised to learn that the Buddhist monastic code regards it as an offence serious enough to merit public confession and public penance. Even in an age when most Catholics considered every act of masturbation a mortal sin—all the more serious if committed by a person who had made a vow of chastity—no more was required of the person who committed it than private confession to a priest.

From the Buddhist point of view, masturbation is an unskillful practice because it manifests and strengthens attachment to sensual pleasure and thus leads to more suffering. The fault is explicitly referred to in the Dhammapada in a passage where the Buddha admonishes a monk who was "in the habit of stimulating himself sexually" and decrees that the bhikkhus abstain from self-induced sensual pleasure, telling them, "This kind of act can lead to suffering."[1]

Even though masturbation does not automatically exclude one from the monastic life, it is considered a serious enough impediment to spiritual progress to demand that the whole community come together to censure the monk who has engaged in it and impose the required weeklong penalty. After penance, a minimum of twenty ordained bhikkhus must assemble and agree that the offending monk is fit to return to his former status. Even if he were to be reinstated to his rank after his public penance, a bhikkhu who was unwilling or believed himself unable to desist from frequent acts of autoeroticism would normally be asked to leave the monastic community.

Contemporary Catholic moral theology has, for the most part, accepted the modern psychological understanding of masturbation as a normal part of the male sexual experience and no longer treats it simply as a moral failing. In the light of a more highly developed understanding of psychosexual development, it is clear that an exclusively moralistic and condemnatory response to masturbation is, in fact, counterproductive. Rather than preventing relapse, condemnation often intensifies feelings of shame and guilt, provoking further acts of masturbation as an expression of self-hatred. In some cases a harsh and judgmental response to the act of masturbation produces a crippling sense of scrupulosity.

On the other hand, contemporary Catholic moral theology does not regard masturbation as morally neutral—that is, little more than a harmless way of releasing pent up sexual energy or nervous tension. The *Catechism of the Catholic Church*, in fact, describes it as a sin "gravely contrary to chastity" (no. 2396).[2]

Masturbation is regarded as an unacceptable form of sexual behavior because Catholic teaching insists on an intrinsic connection between sex and procreation and therefore does not allow for any genital sexual activity outside of marriage. The rationale behind this linkage is explained as follows:

> Both the Magisterium of the Church, in the course of a constant tradition, and the moral sense of the faithful have been in no doubt and have firmly maintained that masturbation is an intrinsically and gravely disordered action. The deliberate use of the sexual faculty, for whatever reason, outside of marriage is essentially contrary to its purpose. For here sexual pleasure is sought outside of the sexual relationship which is demanded by the moral order and in which the total meaning of mutual self-giving and human procreation in the context of true love is achieved. (no. 2352)

It goes on to say, however, that to form an equitable judgment about the subject's moral responsibility and to guide pastoral action, one must take into account such conditions as affective immaturity, force of acquired habit, conditions of anxiety or other psychological or social factors that lessen moral culpability and may even reduce it to a minimum.

Buddhist and Catholic monks agree that what is of utmost importance in dealing with the phenomenon of masturbation is close attention to what is going on in the mind. Masturbation is usually accompanied by a sexual fantasy life that is counterproductive to everything that monastic life stands for. Often these fantasies are about an idealized partner; sometimes they are exploitative, even orgiastic, in character; sometimes they are simply a way of convincing oneself that self-induced sexual release is a necessary and effective way to deal with loneliness, frustration, or insomnia. For this reason the all-important issue to be addressed is how one deals with these fantasies. Rather than denying them, or trying to distract ourselves away from them, or resisting them—tactics that can have the undesired effect of actually increasing our attachment to them—the Buddhist approach is to observe them and place them within the law of *karma*, the law of cause and effect in the ethical realm.

Buddhism teaches that we create karma by our deliberate use of body, speech, and mind. The Buddhist would regard being part of the animal kingdom as a karma consequence. Simply being in the human body means that we are hard-wired for sex. This does not mean that sex is bad; after all, it is necessary for the survival of humans and animals. But in humans it also creates attachment, and attachment ultimately leads to dissatisfaction.

Since the mind is especially important, it is the focus of Buddhist training. If I choose to indulge my sexual fantasies, one of the karma consequences of that choice is that sexual desire will arise again, desire will lead to attachment, and attachment will lead to dukkha. My decision to attend to the fantasy means that my inclination to fantasize will be strengthened and the inclination will gradually turn into a habit.

It is therefore crucial to realize that whenever an image arises in our mind, no matter what it may be, we do have a choice. The practice of meditation teaches us how to be still in the midst of that arising, not seeing these images or thoughts as real or important, and remaining grounded in something much deeper, much more still—compassion and wisdom. If a sexual fantasy arises, we can let it arise and pass without being disturbed, neither trying to make it go away nor indulging it. Every time we allow it to pass without either resisting it or acting on it, a piece of karma consequence has been cleaned up, and the habit energy of indulging in sexual fantasies is diminished.

To the extent that we do not indulge our sexual urges, they diminish. But we should not put much too much stock in waiting for them to go away of their own accord. It is important to bring karma consciousness to this area of our lives: being aware of what arises, being aware of how we are reacting to it, being aware that we do have a choice.

When any kind of compulsion or addiction is involved, we tend to think that choice is no longer operative and that we are compelled to act on the compulsive urge. But such a way of thinking is simply the habit of choosing to identify with the compulsion and to think that it is what is really important. The Buddhist would say that it is necessary to change how we relate to our mind and to the images that arise in it, learning to regard the mind and its images as ultimately unreal and unimportant.

When sexual fantasies arise, we might want to think they are harmless, karma free, and indulge them. But to think in this way would be exceptionally unskillful, for it goes against the law of karma, and the law of karma is not answerable to our personal will. We might wish it were, but part of monastic training is to come to terms with the way things are in the realm of karma, the way the law of cause and effect actually works itself out.

The meditation techniques used by Buddhists train them to recognize that the law of karma is reality and not some unfortunate but arbitrary adversity that intrudes on our life. Understanding how the law of karma applies to the consequences of indulging sexual images and thoughts is key to becoming free of attachment to the sensual pleasure of masturbation and of the disillusion, the dukkha, that is its inevitable consequence.

The Catholic approach to masturbation used to consist in little more than inducing fear by threatening the perpetrator with eternal punishment and insisting that any temptation to "acts of impurity" or "self-abuse" were to be strenuously resisted. Masturbation was sinful because it perverted the end of sex, which was to create life and strengthen the bond between the man and woman responsible for nurturing that new life.

What had been lost in this approach was attention to the way in which the mind produces the thoughts, be they memories or fantasies, that make one turn to autoeroticism as a way to bring about release, and the ease with which repeated acts of masturbation strengthen such unskillful thinking. As Sister Meg Funk put it so well in the title of a book that made the wisdom of John Cassian accessible to modern readers, "thoughts matter."[3]

Giving up sex—or wealth, or honor, or comfort—she goes on to say, is one step in the spiritual path. But one can still be enslaved to thinking about what one has given up and remain stuck. The spiritual wisdom discovered by Antony, the fourth-century father of Western monasticism, speaks to the modern monk as clearly as it did to his contemporaries. He

> realized that his thoughts mattered and that they had to be taken seriously. . . . He began to train himself to notice his thoughts, laying them out, rather than resisting them. . . . to redirect his thoughts, either by rethinking them or by placing a prayer alongside the thought.[4]

Like the Buddha centuries before him, he understood that paying attention to his thoughts was the way to progress toward the freedom, unity, and self-giving love that is the goal of the monastic path.

Like masturbation, pornography—more specifically, the explicit and graphic depiction of human sexual activity—cannot be called a modern phenomenon.[5] Clay figurines from the ancient Near East, frescoes on the walls of Pompeian brothels, sculptures in Hindu temples, and medieval Japanese woodblock prints attest to its long history and its presence across cultures. What is modern is the omnipresence, aggressiveness, and profitability of pornography. In today's world it is a significant component of a free-market economy. According to data provided in early 2007, 12 percent of all websites (4.2 million) were pornographic. Every day there were 68 million search engine requests for pornographic websites—25 percent of all requests. At more than 12 billion dollars annually, porn revenue in the United States is far larger than the combined revenues of ABC, CBS, and NBC. Child pornography alone generated 3 billion dollars annually.[6]

Another significant feature of contemporary pornography is that, thanks to the Internet, it is instantly and anonymously accessible to consumers in the form of high-resolution pictures, videos, and even real-time transmission of people, including minors, performing whatever sexual acts the viewer requests, provided he (and usually it is a he) is willing to pay.[7]

Given the huge profits to be made from pornography, it is only to be expected that those in the business would mount an aggressive propaganda campaign to convince the public that it is harmless and even beneficial. Arguments are made that pornography provides a safety valve for men who might otherwise engage in sexually violent behavior; that women (and men) who allow themselves to be photographed while performing sexual acts are doing what they freely choose to do; that those who use porn recognize it as make-believe and simply enjoy it as a harmless form of entertainment and relaxation.

But this is propaganda pure and simple, created by entrepreneurial pornographers looking to grow their profits or by uncritical proponents of free speech, and then repeated by those who need to justify a behavior that they themselves recognize is dehumanizing for the user and the used. Pornography separates sexuality from emotional intimacy, driving it more and more into the shadowy realms of anonymity, violence, and perversion. It objectifies the human body, making it into little more than an object to be freely exploited for the sexual gratification of the user. It puts forward distorted images of what it means to be a "real man" and a "real woman," an especially worrisome situation given that children between the ages of twelve and seventeen are avid consumers of Internet porn. Pornography can create dependence, demanding more and more time, with the result that those who view it compulsively become less and less interested in productive work and real human relationships.[8]

Pornography can be an especially difficult problem for those who have chosen a celibate way of life. Many—perhaps most— Western monks, Buddhists as well as Catholics, have access to and rely on computers for their education, ministry, and work. Those computers are often to be found in their own rooms or offices. As is the case with any other user, they can be the recipients of unsolicited pornographic e-mail or can unwittingly access a pornographic website while searching for something else. They may initially be repelled by these images, but their curiosity can also be aroused, leading them to go in search of other pornographic sites just "to check them out," an act facilitated by the naïve belief that what they do on their computer is absolutely private. There may also be reasons other than curiosity for accessing online porn, for example, a desire to re-experience, even if virtually, the life one has abandoned; boredom or rebellion; a sense that "just once" won't hurt.

From a monastic point of view, the problem with pornography is that it is one more way of increasing attachment to sensual pleasure and therefore, as the Buddhist would insist, of increasing suffering. The suffering produced by pornography is both immediate and long-term. First comes the anxiety that one will be discovered, followed by the painful awareness of how hypocritically one is acting and the recognition that by the very act of using pornography one is contributing to the depersonalization and exploitation of human sexuality. As one's use of pornography becomes more compulsive, one's appreciation for beauty in all its forms is dulled and often there follows a loss of interest in human interaction and a general coarsening of one's sensibilities.

Once again, what Catholics might learn from Buddhists is how important it is to take notice of one's thoughts and desires, recognizing that it is possible simply to observe them, neither fighting them off nor acting on them, but rather allowing them to rise and to pass. What will be especially helpful for the monk who begins to experience a compulsion to indulge himself in pornographic fantasies is revealing his thoughts to a spiritual counselor who will be able to help him regain his freedom and also help him recognize and accept the ache of loneliness that is an essential element of living celibately.

Like pornography, homosexuality—in the sense of sexual relations with someone of the same sex—is a form of sexual expression that can be found throughout history and across cultures. What is new is the widespread conviction that homosexuality—in the sense of one's sexual orientation—is a given rather than a choice. However, the jury is still out regarding an "essentialist" versus a "constructionist" interpretation of this "given." In other words, there is still no consensus on whether homosexuality is a transhistorical essence or a historical formation.[9]

Also new is the oft-asserted conviction that being "gay" or being "straight" is ultimately what defines a person's identity. For this reason, gay activists encourage "coming out" as an essential element of personal integrity. There appears to be increasingly little recognition of how polymorphous and indiscriminate sexual attraction can be. For example, most people who consider themselves heterosexuals can experience homosexual feelings, though many would be loathe to admit it. As novelist P. D. James observes, "In nearly all close [same-sex] friendships there is a subcutaneous pricking of sexual attraction."[10]

Contemporary Catholic teaching accepts the possibility that one's sexual orientation may not be a condition one chooses, but still regards homosexual acts as "disordered," a most unfortunate term, since it seems to imply that gay people are sick. The reason this term is used in official church documents is because homosexuality is an expression of human sexuality that is "not ordered" to the procreation of life, which, on the basis of what Catholic theology refers to as the Natural Law,[11] is considered to be the fundamental and indispensable purpose for the sexual relationship. Consequently, in line with the Catholic position that restricts genital sexual activity to the relations between husband and wife, homosexual acts are prohibited.[12]

Although many contemporary Buddhists would argue that homosexual relations, per se, were not prohibited by the Buddha, the Vinaya stipulates that a "pandaka" is not to be ordained as a monk, and is to be expelled if he had inadvertently been given ordination. Although the term *pandaka* has been interpreted to encompass a whole range of sexual abnormalities or nonconformist sexual behavior, the narrative context of this section of the Vinaya describes a form of behavior that, in contemporary jargon would be referred to as "hitting on" someone—in other words, soliciting someone for gay sex.

The Vinaya relates that a pandaka who "came to have gone forth among the monks" approached some young monks and said, "Come, venerable ones, commit an offence with me." They refused, as did a number of "large, fat novices" whom he also solicited. Having been rebuffed by his fellow monks, he then approached mahouts and grooms who "committed an offence with him," and then "spread it about, saying, 'These recluses, sons of the Sakyans,[13] are eunuchs, and those of them who are not eunuchs, they too commit offences with eunuchs. Thus they are one and all unchaste.'"

Some monks, having heard what was being said, were understandably distraught about the way the whole monastic order was being vilified and took the matter to the Buddha. His response was, "Monks, if a eunuch is not ordained, he should not be ordained; if he is ordained, he should be expelled."[14]

One commentator on this passage notes that the reason the Buddha ruled against the ordination of pandakas is because—as stated in the commentary—pandakas are "full of passions, unquenchable lust and are dominated by the desire for sex." The term, therefore, designates an effeminate, self-advertising and promiscuous homosexual (the "screaming queen" in popular perception) rather than someone with a homosexual orientation.[15]

Although some Catholic monastic communities would be leery about accepting any self-proclaimed gay person, others distinguish between a candidate's sexual orientation and his behavior. A gay person who gave evidence of psychosexual maturity along with the desire and demonstrated ability to live celibately would be welcomed into many Catholic monastic communities—provided he, like every other novice, was "truly seeking God . . . [and was] zealous for the Work of God, for obedience and humiliations" (RB, ch. 58).

On November 4, 2005, the Vatican's Congregation for Catholic Education published a document entitled "Instruction Concerning the Criteria for the Discernment of Vocations with regard to Persons with Homosexual Tendencies in view of their Admission to the Seminary and to Holy Orders."[16] The document stipulated that men who "practice homosexuality, present deep-seated homosexual tendencies or support the so-called 'gay culture'" cannot be admitted to the seminary or to holy orders. The reason given is that in order to admit a candidate to ordination to the transitional diaconate—at which point he is required to promise celibacy—the church must verify, among other things, that the candidate has reached affective maturity and is able to relate correctly to men and women. The presumption, apparently, is that persons with deep-seated homosexual tendencies do not demonstrate such affective maturity.

One of the general principles for interpreting church law is that restrictive policies are to be interpreted narrowly, while permissive policies are to be interpreted broadly. Since this document restricts the acceptance of candidates to the seminary and to holy orders, it must therefore be interpreted narrowly, and not automatically be interpreted to apply to candidates for monastic life. Furthermore, to equate "deep-seated homosexual tendencies" with a homosexual orientation would be to cast the net far too broadly. What the document is describing is a person whose mind is occupied with homosexual fantasies, who is continually "on the prowl," or always "camping it up"—in other words, a pandaka. Such a person obviously does not demonstrate the qualities one looks for in a candidate for ordination—or, for that matter, for monastic life.

Are men with a homosexual orientation suitable for monastic life? In an essay entitled "Celibacy and the Gift of Gay," one monk, the Trappist Matthew Kelty, proposes that they are, in fact, ideally suited. The basis of his argument is both experiential and theoretical. He identifies himself as a gay celibate monk and turns to Jung for his understanding of the human person as "more than one sex." The usual route for working out the integration of our male and female sides, he says, is in marriage, "where male and female counteract on many levels, and where, hopefully, through exchange, each learns to accept all of the other, all of one's self." [17]

But marriage is not the only way. Some men who very much know themselves to be male will also have so vivid an awareness of their *anima* (to use the Jungian term for the feminine principle) that they do not feel the need for an actual relationship with a woman in order to reach wholeness. They already live with her. These are the people who in large part give a society its poets, its artists, its dreamers, its spiritual guides. In some ways they are on the fringe of society; but in another way, they are right at its very heart, a sign pointing to the integration and unity that is our destiny.

An intense awareness and acceptance of the feminine side of the male (which is not to be confused with effeminacy) is, in Kelty's view, basic to an understanding of what it means to be gay. But the question still remains: How does one deal with this reality, this intense awareness of one's feminine side, this absence of attraction to the feminine outside oneself?

Kelty's point is not that every homosexual must be celibate, but rather that gay men who already sense that they are different from most men, who have a strong religious sense, who seek a point and purpose and a reason to live, and who need love, are ideally suited for the celibate life. [18] In fact, he says, they gravitate toward the celibate religious life since it unites the search for integration and wholeness with a superb direction and purpose.

This is not to say that celibacy will be easy for men who wish to live out their gift of being gay as monks. In the first place, they have been formed by a society that is not generally receptive to men who recognize and do not apologize for their feminine side, nor does it provide much support—moral or material—to those who wish to dedicate their lives to a spiritual quest. In addition, gay men have themselves imbibed the competitive, possessive, self-gratifying spirit that is so characteristic of contemporary Western culture. Add to that the self-hatred and self-contempt that many gay men have internalized because of the hostile environment that has surrounded them, and one can understand how much generosity and *ascesis* will be needed to fashion a community in which they will be able to "anticipate one another in honor; most patiently endure one another's infirmities, whether of body or of character; vie in paying obedience one to another—no one following what he considers useful for himself, but rather what benefits another—[and] tender the charity of brotherhood chastely" (RB, ch. 72).

But in spite of the challenges that face the monk who is gay, Kelty would argue that "being gay is grace indeed in following the celibate way."[19]

Epilogue

In her comprehensive study on the history of celibacy, Elizabeth Abbott observes that it has always been a two-edged sword. As a chosen lifestyle, celibacy may empower and liberate, but when coerced, it can repress and crush. Depending on the reason it is observed, celibacy sustains or torments, emboldens or embitters, protects or humiliates, comforts or punishes.[1]

But celibacy is not the only sexual option that cuts both ways. Throughout the ages, the choice to engage in sexual relations with another person has also been a two-edged sword. For many men and women, a committed sexual relationship has been the path to spiritual and psychological maturity. But it is also obvious that even a freely chosen, committed relationship such as marriage does not always lead to such a positive outcome.

When sexual relationships are promiscuous, the possibility of undesired consequences is even greater. Even though such liaisons may initially be the source of intense physical and emotional pleasure, they almost always bring about the torment of jealousy, distrust, fear, shame, and even revulsion. American pop culture glorifies the unfettered expression of sexuality in its TV shows, music, and tabloids, but it is also replete with stories, both fictional and factual, about people who feel betrayed, wounded, embittered, and, in some few cases, chastened by their forays into sexual freedom.

Abbott is surely right in her insistence that, when coerced, celibacy is rarely a path to psychosexual maturity or spiritual growth. However, even those who have freely chosen celibacy— or consented to *being chosen* by celibacy—do not necessarily feel sustained, emboldened, protected, or comforted by the life they live—at least not all the time. Thomas Merton gives eloquent voice to the experience of many who are convinced that celibacy is the path most suited for them, but can still be tormented, even embittered, by doubt and loneliness.

While celibacy inevitably involves loneliness, it must also be noted that celibates are not the only people who feel lonely. Matthew Kelty remarks that it's not their loneliness that makes monks particularly different; it's what they do with their loneliness that makes them, he suggests, "somewhat different."[2]

What the monk, Buddhist or Catholic, does with his celibate loneliness—or perhaps it would be more accurate to say: what he in his best moments wants and tries to do with his celibate loneliness—is observe it, name it, feel it, lament it, accept it as an essential element of being human, and ultimately give thanks for it and draw on it as a resource for spiritual growth.

Loneliness invites the Catholic monk to enter into a deeper relationship with the God who, in Saint Augustine's words, is *interior intimo meo*, the God who is closer to me than I am to myself. Celibacy can also allow the monk to enter into a deeper and more mature relationship with other people, freed from the craving for pleasure or self-interest that is such a common, even if unintended and unrecognized, component of most friendships. Provided he does not deny or flee from his loneliness, he will come to understand that while love for God and neighbor is at the very heart of the Christian life, the monk's way of loving freely is to forego the genital expression of that love along with the attachment it produces.

A demythologized celibacy is not a devalued celibacy. Rather, it is a way of life whose value can be more clearly understood when it is seen not as some kind of angelic life that is possible only for a privileged few, nor as an unrealizable ideal, but as an option that, for any number of reasons, ordinary people may be attracted to.

For some of these "ordinary people" celibacy may have no religious meaning at all; they simply do not want to be tied down, and they are clear-sighted enough to know that a sexual relationship, even outside of "wedlock," creates a bond. For others, the choice for celibacy goes hand in hand with their desire to concentrate their energy on a spiritual journey, be that the inner journey of self-understanding or a deepened relationship with God, or the more outward but still spiritual journey of serving one's neighbor with unselfish love.

For these people, Buddhist or Catholic, monk or lay, celibacy is not so much a "charism" as a "skillful means" for realizing their humanity and their destiny, which ultimately consists in becoming free from self-centered desire in order to draw nearer to lasting peace and happiness.

As this book was nearing completion one of my monastic brothers told me of a high school classmate of ours who had called to ask for prayers. He was about to have a double hip replacement, but was even more concerned for the well-being of his wife during the time he would be in the hospital. She was in an advanced stage of multiple sclerosis and relied on him as her primary caregiver. Their children were able to arrange their schedules to insure that someone would always be with her while he was in the hospital and during his convalescence. But what would happen if the operation did not produce the hoped-for results and he was no longer able to care for her? His anxiety about the future was overwhelming him.

In the course of his conversation he remarked, "You monks have it good."

Indeed we do. Celibacy joined to life in community offers monks a freedom from anxiety and a freedom for spiritual practice that is simply not possible for those who have accepted the responsibilities, the joys, and the trials of marriage. This awareness should be cause for both thanksgiving and renewed dedication to spiritual practice and service of others.

Appendix

Father Thomas Ryan, a member of the Paulist Fathers and advisor to Monastic Interreligious Dialogue, participated in Monks in the West II and wrote the following report for MID's online Bulletin (#77). Father Ryan is director of the Paulist Office of Ecumenical and Interfaith Relations in New York City.

The electronic sign at the Minneapolis/Saint Paul airport was flashing "Orange Alert" as a dozen Buddhist monks arrived in their burnt-orange robes from around the country. They were on their way to Saint John's Abbey in Collegeville, Minnesota, for three days of dialogue on celibacy with a similar number of Catholic monastics.

As he opened the October 26–29 meeting, Father William Skudlarek, executive director of Monastic Interreligious Dialogue (MID), said "You (Buddhists) have been at this for some five to seven hundred years longer than we have. We have something to learn."

This was the second Monks in the West interreligious dialogue; the first took place in 2004 at the City of Ten Thousand Buddhas in northern California. On the Catholic side, the participants came from Saint John's Abbey, five other Benedictine monasteries and one Trappist monastery. The twelve Buddhists represented the Theravada, Mahayana, and Tibetan traditions.

The first session dealt with Theory, the "why" of celibacy. Buddhist participants explained that their teachings focus on

seeing how suffering is created and cured. Attachments give rise
to suffering, so advancement in the spiritual life requires letting
go of one's attachments. Attachment to desires, among which
are sexual desires, is a hindrance to spiritual progress.

"Raging desire takes away choice, freedom," said Reverend
Kusala Bhikshu, resident monk at the International Buddhist
Meditation Center in Los Angeles, in his opening presentation.
"The senses must be controlled in order to be free."

Brother Gregory Perron from Saint Procopius Monastery in
Illinois spoke of how monastic life demands a profound understanding and acceptance of solitude. "Celibacy is a tool," offered
Perron, "a skillful means like intentional simplicity of life, by
which our heart is burrowed out and the core of our being laid
bare. By embracing it, the monk accepts the aloneness that characterizes every human being."

In response to Buddhist reflections on the illusory nature of
the body, Catholic participants pointed out Christianity's re-
markably positive evaluation of the body in the doctrines of the
Incarnation, bodily Resurrection and Ascension of Jesus, and the
indwelling of the Holy Spirit.

Both sides acknowledged balancing points of reference as
well, such as, in Christianity, Paul's "Who will deliver me from
this body of death?" (Rom 7:24); and, in Buddhism, the teaching
that humankind, while fifth from the bottom in the thirty-one
realms of its cosmology, is the only one in which spiritual growth
can happen. Thus human form is, in the end, praised by the
Buddha.

In the second session the participants moved from Theory
to Practice. Reverend Jisho Perry from Shasta Buddhist Abbey
in California said that "the whole thrust of training is not to give
in to desire that arises." He described the Buddhist method of
accepting sexual feelings without either acting on them or re-
pressing them, but just letting them pass through. "The right use
of will is willingness, not will power—the willingness to sit
there and let that feeling pass through," he said.

Father Skudlarek expressed appreciation for the Buddhist
approach to transforming the sexual energy. "Our training did

not teach us to accept sexual feelings with awareness and then let them pass without acting on them. You had to fight them! And the more you resisted, the stronger they got!"

Reverend Heng Sure who teaches at the Graduate Theological Union in Berkeley, presented celibacy as the first step in a three-step process that goes from celibacy to stillness to insight. "It should not be seen just as a difficult adjunct to the spiritual path, but as essential to it," he said.

The practice of meditation calls for daily periods when the senses are stilled and not allowed to pursue sense objects. "Something happens to the energy in the stillness," said Heng Sure; "the pressure goes away." In married life, he explained, spiritual practice is "partial and piecemeal," making celibacy a more effective means to move toward insight, and the peace and happiness that flow from it.

In the discussion, Father Mark Serna, president of MID, pointed out that "in Christianity married people can be holy, too; one doesn't have to be celibate to go to heaven."

Catholic monks emphasized how, in Christian faith, motivation for celibacy is strongly relational. "For me," said Father Terrance Kardong of Assumption Abbey in North Dakota, "it's the deep personal relationship with Jesus that enables me to do something this hard." Father Michael Peterson from Blue Cloud Abbey in South Dakota drew a laugh when he shared, "When some college kids asked me: 'How can you live without sex?' an answer came that I wasn't even planning on: 'God's a better kisser.' In celibacy I transfer my desire for fulfillment to God."

Heng Sure said that the idea of embracing celibacy because it leads to love is not a Buddhist approach. "A Buddhist would say, 'it leads to liberation from further suffering—both personal and, in the Bodhisattva path, for everyone.'"

Lama Norbu added that the relational dimension, while not highlighted in the Buddhist practice of celibacy, is not absent either. "Monks choose to live in community," he said. "And the core of their spirituality is compassion for others."

The third session focused on how the two traditions handle transgressions and failure. Ajahn Punnadhammo from Ontario delineated the "Four Defeats" in Buddhist monasticism—sexual intercourse, stealing above a trivial amount, killing a human being, and falsely claiming superior spiritual achievements— and explained how, if a monk should do any of these four actions, he is no longer a monk and is not allowed to be readmitted into the community. Responses to lesser sexual infractions are spelled out in detail in the monastic code.

Buddhists listened with keen interest to Abbot John Klassen of Saint John's Abbey as he related how, in response to the exposure of sexual misconduct by Catholic clergy and religious, the bishops ruled that transgressions against minors could result in expulsion from the priesthood.

But, said Klassen, "leaders of religious communities took a fundamentally different stance. They had to agree to remove any offender from ministry, but they were not willing to throw them out of the community. They agreed to do risk assessment and develop supervision for offenders. Offenders have understood that because of recidivism and lack of public trust, supervision plans are necessary."

Klassen described how, in the 1970s, "our awareness of failures moved from the moral arena to the psychological arena, and now to the awareness that the sexual abuse of minors is a crime. New guidelines provide a level of behavioral specificity that we've never seen before."

In the closing session, the monks discussed both what contributes and detracts from the development of friendship and healthy intimacy in celibate communities.

Through the event, participants began the day with an hour of quiet sitting in meditation, and joined the monastic community at Saint John's for their rhythm of daily prayer.

At the end, Lama Norbu passed around Buddhist prayer flags for all the participants to sign. "I will return to Tibet next summer," he said, "and erect these flags on the highest mountain in the world where the dedicated energies of those here and all the communities they represent will fly up to heaven."

Thomas Ryan, CSP

Notes

Introduction—pp. v–xi

1. Garden City, NY: Doubleday, 1971.
2. Ibid., p. 11. Greeley's note expands on the way "myth" has been used among historians of religion, literary critics, and social scientists: "To say that Jesus is a myth is not to say that he is a legend but that his life and message are an attempt to demonstrate 'the inner meaning of the universe and of human life.' As Charles Long puts it, a myth points to the definite manner in which the world is available for man: 'The word and content of myth are revelations of power.' Or as A. K. Coomaraswamy observes, 'Myth embodies the nearest approach to absolute truth that can be stated in words.' "
3. A news release written by one of the participants, Fr. Thomas Ryan, CSP, can be found on pp. 94–97.
4. See, for example, Raimundo Panikkar, *Blessed Simplicity: The Monk as Universal Archetype* (New York: Seabury Press, 1982).
5. The parallel passage in the Gospel of Luke adds "or wife" (18:29).
6. Columba Stewart, *Cassian the Monk* (New York: Oxford University Press, 1998), 62.

Chapter 1—pp. 1–16

1. Or, as Anselm Grün puts it, "Benedict's community is not a bachelor's club dedicated to its own thriving. . . . It is a mature community, one in which individuals very deliberately face their solitariness and maintain it before God." *Benedict of Nursia: His Message for Today*, trans. Linda M. Maloney (Collegeville, MN: Liturgical Press, 2006), 60.

2. A. L. De Silva, "Homosexuality and Theravada Buddhism," http://www.budsas.org/ebud/ebdha100.htm (accessed November 14, 2007). The chapter is part of the website "BuddhaSasana A Buddhist Page by Bihn Anson."

3. T. S. Eliot, THE DRY SALVAGES (No. 3 of 'Four Quartets').

4. "In Christ" or similar expressions, e.g., "in Jesus," "in him," "in the love of Christ," occur frequently in the letters of Saint Paul.

5. The expression is Eugene Boylan's in *This Tremendous Lover* (Cork, Ireland: The Mercier Press, 1946), 296. It was inspired, he said, by Saint Augustine's Tractate 108 on the Gospel of John, where he comments on Jesus' words "And for them do I sanctify myself" as follows: "[I sanctify] them in myself as though I am sanctifying myself, because in me they themselves, too, are myself." St. Augustine, *Tractates on the Gospel of John 55–111*, trans. John W. Rettig (Washington D.C.: The Catholic University of America Press, 1994), 282. Earlier in the same Tractate, Augustine had said, "Those about whom he says this, as I said, are his members, and the Head and the body is the one Christ . . ." (281).

6. In William O. Paulsell, *Letters from a Hermit. With Letters from Matthew Kelty, O.C.S.O.* (Springfield, IL: Templegate Publishers, 1978), 123f.

7. "The thing everybody has to remember is that the monastery is a place where withdrawal is honored and respected and, most of all, preserved. But it's a notion of withdrawal, not desertion. The monk is a lover. He may hate the ways of the world, but he loves the people. His prayer is not for himself. It's for—and with—everyone." Frank Bianco, *Voices of Silence* (New York: Paragon House, 1991), 203.

8. The Rule of Benedict, ch. 1.

9. The literal meaning of the Buddhist word for monk—*bhikkhu* or *bhikshu*—is beggar.

10. "Interpretare vocabulum Monachi, hoc est nomen tuum. Quid facis in turba qui solus es?" *Epistola XIV ad Heliodorum Monachum*, in Sancti Eusebii Hieronymi *Opera Omnia*, ed. J. P. Migne, *Patrologiae Latinae*, vol. XXII (Paris, 1845; rpt.: Turnholt, Brepols, 1986), 350.

11. "Quare ergo et nos non appellemus monachos, cum dicit psalmus: ECCE QUAM BONUM ET QUAM IUCUNDUM HABITARE FRATRES IN UNUM? Μόνος enim unus dicitur, et non unus quomodocumque. Nam et in turba est unus, sed una com multis; unus dici potest, μόνος non potest, id est solus; μόνος enim unus solus est. Qui ergo sic vivunt in unum ut unum hominem faciant, ut sit illis vere, quomodo scriptum

est, *una anima et unum cor*—multa corpora, sed non multae animae; multa corpora, sed non multa corda—recte dicitur μόνος, id est unus solus." Augustinus, *Enarrationes in Psalmos 119–133*, ed. Franco Gori. Corpus Scriptorum Ecclesiasticorum Latinorum, vol. XCV/3 (Vienna: Verlag der Österreichischen Akademie der Wissenschaften, 2001), 327.

12. The literal meaning of the word is "healers."

13. *Dionysius the Pseudo-Areopagite: The Ecclesiastical Hierarchy*, trans. Thomas L. Campbell (Lanham, MD: University Press of America, 1981), VI, 1, 3.

14. Thomas Merton, "Preface to the Japanese Edition of *THOUGHTS IN SOLITUDE* March 1966," in *Honorable Reader*, ed. Robert E. Daggy (New York: Crossroad, 1989), 111.

15. Anselm Grün, *Celibacy—A Fullness of Life*, trans. Gregory Roettger and Luise R. Pugh (Schuyler, NE: BMH Publications, 1993), 13.

16. *Dionysius*, VI, 3, 2.

17. Merton, *Honorable Reader*, 116.

18. 3.6.11.

19. Thomas Merton, *Disputed Questions* (New York: Farrar, Strauss and Cudahy, 1960), 180.

20. Nancy Klein Maguire, *An Infinity of Little Hours. Five Young Men and Their Trial of Faith in the Western World's Most Austere Monastic Order* (New York: Public Affairs, 2006).

21. *Letters from a Hermit*, 59–60.

22. Matthew Kelty, "Desolation Row." A retreat conference given at Gethsemani, January 1970. http://www.bardstown.com/~brchrys/homilies/mkDesRow.htm (accessed November 14, 2007).

23. See the Appendix, page 94.

24. *The Diary of a Young Girl: The Definitive Edition*, ed. Otto H. Frank and Mirjam Pressler (New York: Doubleday, 1991), 156.

Chapter 2—pp. 17–35

1. Michael Mott, *The Seven Mountains of Thomas Merton* (Boston: Houghton Mifflin, 1984).

2. Amazon.com notes that Merton's biography is cited in 453 other books.

3. This and other documents of Vatican II are easily accessed on the Vatican website: http://www.vatican.va (accessed November 14, 2007). Click on "Resource Library."

4. The breadth and depth of his interests are well documented in William Apel, *The Interfaith Letters of Thomas Merton* (Maryknoll, NY: Orbis Books, 2006).

5. Thomas Merton, *Learning to Love: Exploring Solitude and Freedom.* The Journals of Thomas Merton, vol. 6, ed. Christine M. Bochen (HarperSanFrancisco, 1997), 92. The journal entry was made on July 8, 1966. Henceforward, most references to this volume of Merton's journals will simply be indicated by noting in the text the date on which an entry was made.

6. Ibid., 341. This citation is from Appendix A, "A Midsummer Diary for M." The entry date is June 23, 1966.

7. Thomas Merton, *The Intimate Merton: His Life from His Journals*, ed. Patrick Hart and Jonathan Montaldo (HarperSanFrancisco, 1999), xii.

8. She is referred to as "S." in Mott's biography.

9. John Howard Griffin, *Follow the Ecstasy: The Hermitage Years of Thomas Merton*, ed. Robert Bonazzi (Maryknoll, NY: Orbis Books, 1993). "For Griffin, a man devoted to the integrity of privacy, [revealing the identity of M.] was a difficult decision. How to tell the truth as Merton had told it without sensationalism and to avoid demeaning Margie Smith's own right to privacy? In an extended series of dialogue with James Laughlin (Merton's longtime friend and publisher at New Directions, who was also one of the three trustees of the Merton Legacy Trust) and Father Flavian Burns (Merton's Abbot at Gethsemani and a valued friend of the monk), Griffin weighed every aspect of the question. During that same period, Margie Smith was in correspondence with Laughlin, and she made no objections to Griffin writing an interpretation of the facts. By that time, she had moved to another part of the country and was sharing a happy life with her new husband" (Foreword, xii).

10. "The second kind [of monks] are the Anchorites or Hermits: those who, no longer in the first fervor of the reformation, but after long probation in a monastery, having learned by the help of many brethren how to fight against the devil, go out well armed from the ranks of the community to the solitary combat of the desert (*ad singulam pugnam eremi*)." RB, ch. 1.

11. There are remarkable similarities between Merton's description of his struggle to remain faithful to the life he had chosen and the admission of the celebrated French priest, Father Henri-Antoine Groues, better known as "Abbé Pierre," admired throughout the world as a tireless advocate of the homeless and marginalized. Two years before

his death in 2007 he published *Mon Dieu . . . Pourquoi?* a set of reflections in which he acknowledged that he had broken his vow of celibacy.
"It happened that every now and then, I fell," he wrote. "I never had
regular relationships, because I never allowed sexual desire to put
down roots. I've known the experience of sexual desire and its occasional fulfillment, but this fulfillment was in truth a source of dissatisfaction, because I never felt sincere. . . . I've understood that in order
to be fully satisfied, sexual desire needs to express itself in a sentimen-
tal relationship, tender, trusting. That kind of relationship was denied
to me by my choice of life. I would have only made both the woman
and myself unhappy, tormented between two irreconcilable options for
my life." Quoted by John L. Allen Jr., in "All Things Catholic," posted
online on the *National Catholic Reporter* website on January 26, 2007 (vol.
6, no. 61).

12. Thomas Merton, *Dancing in the Water of Life: Seeking Peace in the
Hermitage*. The Journals of Thomas Merton, vol. 5, ed. Robert E. Daggy
(HarperSanFrancisco, 1997).

13. Thomas Merton, *The Other Side of the Mountain: The End of the
Journey*. The Journals of Thomas Merton, vol. 7, ed. Patrick Hart, O.C.S.O.
(HarperSanFrancisco, 1998).

14. Thomas Merton, "Notes on Love," *Frontier* 10 (Autumn 1967):
211–14.

15. Thomas Merton, *Thoughts in Solitude* (New York: Farrar, Straus
& Cudahy, 1956, 1958).

16. The preface can be found in Thomas Merton, *Honorable Reader:
Reflections on My Work*, ed. Robert E. Daggy (New York: Crossroad,
1989), 107–18.

17. Griffin, *Follow the Ecstasy*, 56.

18. Thomas Merton, *Witness to Freedom. The Letters of Thomas Merton
in Times of Crisis*. Selected and edited by William H. Shannon (New
York: Farrar Straus Giroux, 1994), 238–39.

19. Thomas Merton, *The Springs of Contemplation: A Retreat at the
Abbey of Gethsemani*, ed. Jane Marie Richardson. First published by Farrar, Straus & Giroux, Inc., 1992 (Notre Dame IN: Ave Maria Press, 1997),
179.

20. The *Dhammapada* (The Words of Truth) is a collection of 423
verses in Pali uttered by the Buddha on some 305 different occasions.

21. Thomas Merton, *Cassian and the Fathers: Initiation into the Monastic Traditio*, ed. Patrick F. O'Connell (Kalamazoo MI: Cistercian Publications, 2005), 114.

Chapter 3—pp. 36–49

1. This and other encyclicals (from Pope Leo XIII [1878–1903] to the present) are easily accessed on the Vatican website: http://www .vatican.va (accessed November 14, 2007). Click on "Papal Archive."

2. Beatification is the penultimate step in the process of officially declaring someone to be a saint.

3. Benedict XVI, *Deus caritas est*. Online at the Vatican website: www .vatican.va (accessed November 14, 2007).

4. A controverted phrase, to say the least. A common interpretation in Christian churches in both the East and the West is that adultery is legitimate grounds for divorce. The Roman Catholic Church interprets "except for unchastity" more strictly to mean an incestuous marriage that is *de facto* invalid.

5. Sam Roberts, "51% of Women Are Now Living Without Spouse," New York *Times*, January 16, 2007. The author provides the following breakdown: "Among the more than 117 million women over the age of 15, according to the marital status category in the Census Bureau's latest American Community Survey, 63 million are married. Of those, 3.1 million are legally separated and 2.4 million said their husbands were not living at home for one reason or another.

"That brings the number of American women actually living with a spouse to 57.5 million, compared with the 59.9 million who are single or whose husbands were not living at home when the survey was taken in 2005."

6. Stephen Thompson, "Wedding Day Blues: Finding the Perfect Mix CD." National Public Radio, Morning Edition, June 19, 2007. http:// www.npr.org/templates/story/story.php?storyId=11157882 (accessed November 14, 2007).

Chapter 4—pp. 50–66

1. James A. Wiseman, "Thomas Merton and Theravada Buddhism," in *Merton & Buddhism: Wisdom, Emptiness & Everyday Mind*, ed. Bonnie Bowman Thurston (Louisville KY: Fons Vitae, 2007), 31f.

2. After receiving the Bhikshu/Bhikkhu Pratimoksha Rules, monks in the Mahayana tradition receive the Ten Major and Forty-eight Subsidiary Bodhisattva Precepts of the Bodhisattva Rules. These rules come from the "Net of Brahma" Sutra, a Mahayana text, and thus are not shared by the Theravada tradition. They are, however, central to the

Bodhisattva Path. Monks in both the Theravada and the Mahayana traditions formally recite their rules every fortnight.

3. Vinaya Pitaka: http://www.accesstoinsight.org/lib/authors/thanissaro/bmc1/ch04.html (accessed November 14, 2007).

4. Thich Nhat Hanh, *Freedom Wherever We Go. A Buddhist Monastic Code for the Twenty-first Century* (Berkeley: Parallax Press, 2004), 34.

5. Vinaya Pitaka: http://www.accesstoinsight.org/lib/authors/thanissaro/bmc1/ch05.html (accessed November 14, 2007).

6. Vinaya Pitaka: http://www.dhammaweb.net/Tipitaka/vinaya .php?page=6 (accessed November 14, 2007).

7. Verse 202. *The Dhammapada*, ed. K. Sri Dhammananda (Kuala Lampur: Sasana Abhiwurdhi Wardhana Society, 1988), 403.

8. Verse 215. Ibid., 415.

9. The reason for this and the following guideline is that the monks wore no briefs under their tunics.

10. See *Pachomian Koinonia*, vol. II, *Pachomian Chronicles and Rules*, trans. Armand Veilleux (Kalamazoo MI: Cistercian Studies, 1981), 145–79 passim.

11. *The Rule of the Master*, trans. Luke Eberle (Kalamazoo MI: Cistercian Publications, 1977), Ch. xi, "The Deans of the Monastery."

12. Anselm Grün, *Celibacy—A Fullness of Life*, 25.

13. Elizabeth Abbott, *A History of Celibacy* (New York: Scribner, 1999), 87.

14. The "Rule of our holy Father Basil"—actually two rules for monks, known as the *Longer Rule* and the *Shorter Rule*—on the other hand, has very little that specifically deals with sexuality. What Basil's Rule does offer, however, is an emphasis on moderation and charity: "[Basil] was confronted with the ascetic excesses of the Eustathian movement. Nor had he any need to insist on solitude, virginity, continual prayer and other things of this nature. On the contrary, he had to moderate the fervour of these people by pointing out to them the demands of charity and community life as described in the New Testament." Mayeul de Dreuille, *Seeking the Absolute Love: the Founders of Christian Monasticism* (New York: Crossroad, 1999), 52.

15. Stewart, *Cassian the Monk*, 62.

16. Ibid., 63.

17. Ibid., 75.

18. Thomas Merton, *Cassian and the Fathers*, 164.

19. Conference XII, 15. *Cassian on Chastity: Institute VI, Conference XII, Conference XXII*. Introduction and translation by Terrence Kardong

(Richardton, ND: Assumption Abbey Press, 1993), 47. Regarding the restriction of sleep to three or four hours, Stewart notes, "Nothing establishes purity, Cassian claims, as well as nocturnal vigilance (*Inst.* 6.23)" (*Cassian the Monk*, 74). The reason for this, at least in part, is that a monk who had been keeping vigil for most of the night would probably fall asleep the moment his head hit the pillow, saving him from the temptation to masturbate as he was trying to get to sleep.

20. Stewart, *Cassian the Monk*, 73.

21. See Romans 7:7: "Yet, if it had not been for the law, I would not have known sin."

22. Lauren Pristas, "The Theological Anthropology of John Cassian." Ph.D. diss., Boston College, 1993 (Ann Arbor MI: UMI Dissertation Services), 267.

23. Ibid., 54.

24. "Blessed are the pure in heart, for they will see God" (Matt 5:8).

Chapter 5—pp. 67–78

1. See Lauren Slater, "Love, the Thing Called Love," *National Geographic* (February 2006): 35.

2. The statement of a vowed religious highlights the illogicality of this position: "I publicly professed three vows and, quite frankly, have violated all of them as I've grown into deeper understanding of myself in relation to those vows. What I fail to understand is why no one seems to get upset that I've been self-willed or have found ways to 'procure' spending money while they have become hysterical over the fact that I've loved deeply and have expressed it physically. Understand, I'm not talking about flaunting any of the vows; I *am* talking about the double standard of being permitted to 'grow' into two of them while not being permitted to budge at all in the third." In Sheila Murphy, *A Delicate Dance: Sexuality, Celibacy, and Relationships among Catholic Clergy and Religious* (New York: Crossroad, 1992), 120.

3. See above, p. 57.

4. The penal code of Benedict's Rule comprises chapters 23 to 30.

5. Available on the website of the United States Conference of Catholic Bishops: www.usccb.org/ click on "Church Documents" and then on "The Charter" (accessed November 14, 2007).

6. The *Charter for the Protection of Children and Young People* accompanying the *Essential Norms* notes that the age is to be raised from six-

teen to eighteen years, the age of majority in the United States since 1994.

7. *Essential Norms*, n. 2.

8. Ibid., n. 1. The abbot of a monastic community would be such a "major superior."

9. Available on the CMSM website: http://www.cmsm.org/ (accessed November 14, 2007).

10. December 23, 2003. © Praesidium Inc., June 2001.

11. ". . . unless it is a specific job requirement and the Member is trained to discuss these matters [and] the conversations are part of a legitimate lesson and discussion for teenagers regarding human sexuality issues."

12. See RB, ch. 2, "What Kind of Man the Abbot Ought to Be"; ch. 27, "How Solicitous the Abbot Should Be for the Excommunicated," and ch. 64, "On Constituting an Abbot"; ch. 73, "On the Fact that the Full Observance of Justice Is not Established in This Rule."

Chapter 6—pp. 79–90

1. From the story appended to verse 117.

2. The *Catechism* is easily accessible on the Vatican website: www.vatican.va (accessed November 14, 2007). Click on "Resource Library."

3. Mary Margaret Funk, *Thoughts Matter: The Practice of Spiritual Life* (New York: Continuum, 1998).

4. Ibid., 15.

5. It is generally held that the term "pornography" in the sense of a specific genre of written material or images specifically intended to sexually stimulate the reader or viewer is a creation of the Victorian age. Ancient depictions of sexually explicit scenes may have been intended for use in religious fertility rituals.

6. These data are taken from http://familysafemedia.com/pornography_statistics.html (accessed November 14, 2007).

7. In December 2006 the *New York Times* published a detailed report on how a thirteen-year-old boy with a webcam was lured into selling images of his body on the Internet over the course of five years: Kurt Eichenwald, "Through His Webcam, a Boy Joins a Sordid Online World," *New York Times*, December 19, 2005.

8. There is no consensus on whether or not it is accurate to speak of "addiction" to pornography. One of the reasons for the ongoing debate is that while drug addicts need increasingly larger doses to get

high, it does not seem to be true that those "addicted" to porn need to see more and more extreme material to feel the same level of excitement they first experienced. However, even those who question the appropriateness of describing problems with pornography as an addiction agree that viewing pornography can become a compulsive behavior.

9. See Stephen D. Moore, *God's Beauty Parlor and Other Queer Spaces in and around the Bible* (Stanford, CA: Stanford University Press, 2001), 15. On the constructionist/essentialist debate generally, Moore refers to *Forms of Desire: Sexual Orientation and the Social Constructionist Controversy*, edited by Edward Stein (New York: Routledge, 1992).

10. P. D. James, *Children of Men* (New York: Alfred A. Knopf, Inc., 1992), 13.

11. "The natural law is written and engraved in the soul of each and every man, because it is human reason ordaining him to do good and forbidding him to sin. . . . But this command of human reason would not have the force of law if it were not the voice and interpreter of a higher reason to which our spirit and our freedom must be submitted." Leo XIII, *Libertas praestantissimum*, 597, quoted in the *Catechism of the Catholic Church*, no. 1954.

12. "Homosexuality refers to relations between men or between women who experience an exclusive or predominant sexual attraction toward persons of the same sex. It has taken a great variety of forms through the centuries and in different cultures. Its psychological genesis remains largely unexplained. Basing itself on Sacred Scripture, which presents homosexual acts as acts of grave depravity, tradition has always declared that 'homosexual acts are intrinsically disordered.' They are contrary to the natural law. They close the sexual act to the gift of life. They do not proceed from a genuine affective and sexual complementarity. Under no circumstances can they be approved.

"The number of men and women who have deep-seated homosexual tendencies is not negligible. This inclination, which is objectively disordered, constitutes for most of them a trial. They must be accepted with respect, compassion, and sensitivity. Every sign of unjust discrimination in their regard should be avoided. These persons are called to fulfill God's will in their lives and, if they are Christians, to unite to the sacrifice of the Lord's Cross the difficulties they may encounter from their condition.

"Homosexual persons are called to chastity. By the virtues of self-mastery that teach them inner freedom, at times by the support of disinterested friendship, by prayer and sacramental grace, they can and should gradually and resolutely approach Christian perfection." *Catechism of the Catholic Church*, paragraphs 2357–2359.

13. The historical Buddha, Siddhartha Gautama, is also known as Sakyamuni or Shakyamuni ("sage of the Shakyas").

14. *Mahavagga*, I, 61. In *The Book of the Discipline (Vinaya-Pitaka)*, Vol. IV *(Mahavagga)*. Trans. I. B. Horner (London: Luzac & Company, 1971), 109. The word "eunuch" here appears to be a synonym for pandaka.

15. A. L. De Silva, "Homosexuality and Theravada Buddhism," http://www.budsas.org/ebud/ebdha100.htm (accessed November 14, 2007). The chapter is part of the website "BuddhaSasana A Buddhist Page by Bihn Anson."

16. Available on the Vatican website: http://www.vatican.va/ (accessed November 14, 2007).

17. In Matthew Kelty, *My Song Is of Mercy*, ed. Michael Downey (New York: Sheed & Ward, 1994), 256. Kelty makes the same argument in the chapter "The Monastic Influence," from *Flute Solo*, which is also included in this collection of his works (42–47).

18. Kelty explicitly notes that if he does not deal with the question of celibacy for women, "it is for lack of experience and knowledge, not for lack of courtesy or concern" (*My Song Is of Mercy*, 259).

19. Kelty, *My Song Is of Mercy*, 257.

Epilogue—pp. 91–93

1. Elizabeth Abbott, *A History of Celibacy*, 426.

2. Matthew Kelty. In William O. Paulsell, *Letters from a Hermit. With Letters from Matthew Kelty, O.C.S.O.* (Springfield IL: Templegate Publishers, 1978), 12.

Glossary

(Note: When two terms are given—for example, Bhikkhu/Bhikshu—the first is in Pali, the second in Sanskrit.)

Arhat
In Theravada, a person who has practiced monastic disciplines and reached nirvana.

Bhikkhu/Bhikshu
A Buddhist monk.

Bhikkhuni/Bhikshuni
A Buddhist nun.

Bodhisattva
In Mahayana Buddhism, one who compassionately postpones final enlightenment for the sake of others.

Buddha
See Shakyamuni Buddha.

Canon Law
The authoritative church laws concerning procedures and discipline that are to be observed by Roman Catholics.

Cenobite
A monk who lives in community.

Celibacy
The state of life assumed by a monk/nun (and, in the Catholic Church, by a priest) in which one promises to refrain from marriage and any sexual relations in order to devote oneself entirely to the spiritual life.

Chan
A major and influential school of Chinese Mahayana Buddhism that emphasizes meditation as a way to enlightenment (known as Son in Korea and Zen in Japan).

Chastity
As used by Catholics, chastity means appropriate sexual behavior, i.e., monogamous relations in marriage; no sexual (genital) activity outside of marriage.

Dhammapada
"The path of the Dhamma"; 423 verses in Pali uttered by the Buddha on some 305 occasions for the benefit of a wide range of human beings.

Dhamma/Dharma
A term used by both Hindus and Buddhists that can mean truth, law, order, duty, or thing, as well as the teaching of the Buddha.

Dukkha
Buddhist term for the "dissatisfactory" condition of human existence. Often translated "suffering."

Kamma/Karma
A doctrine common to Hinduism and Buddhism that holds that one's state in this life is the result of physical and mental actions in past incarnations, and that present action can determine one's destiny in future incarnations or rebirths. The working of the Law of Cause and Effect, or "As you sow, so shall you reap."

Koan
A story, dialogue, question, or statement in the history and lore of Chan (Zen) Buddhism, generally containing elements that are

inaccessible to rational understanding, but accessible to intuition. They are often used by Zen practitioners as objects of meditation to induce an experience of enlightenment or realization, and by Zen teachers as testing questions to validate a student's experience of enlightenment.

Mahayana

"The Great Vehicle"; also the "Northern Tradition." One of the three major traditions of Buddhism. It emerged as a major tradition around the second century and spread to East Asia: China, Korea, Japan, and Vietnam. It added more scriptures to the canon, presenting the Buddha's teachings from a more nondualistic view of reality.

Nibbana/Nirvana

Hinduism: a blowing out, or extinction, of the flame of life through reunion with Brahma.
Buddhism: the state of perfect blessedness achieved by the extinction of all passions and desires. Union with the absolute.

Pali

The language in which the earliest scriptures of Buddhism were recorded; the religious textual language used by Theravada Buddhism.

Parajika

"Defeat." One of four transgressions which automatically strip a bhikkhu of his monastic status.

Patimokkha/Pratimoksha

"Disciplinary Code." The name of the code of monks' rules, which on all full-moon and new-moon days is recited before the assembled community of fully ordained monks.

Pelagianism

The heretical theological view of the British monk Pelagius (354–420) who taught that humans can achieve salvation through their own sustained efforts.

Religious
A member of a religious order who is bound by vows of poverty, chastity, and obedience.

Rule of Benedict
A monastic code and monastic spiritual teaching written in Italy around the year 529 and gradually becoming the rule of life for all monastic men and women in the Western Christian Church.

Samadhi
State of mind characterized by intense concentration and freedom from distraction and goals, in which the essential nature of the self can be experienced directly.

Sangha
The Buddhist monastic community or, more broadly, the community of Buddhist practitioners.

Sanghadisesa
"Meeting of the Sangha." Used to describe a level of transgression that demands a meeting of the sangha to impose a public penance on the monk who has transgressed.

Sanskrit
The classical sacerdotal or religious language of ancient India in which most of its texts were transmitted. It is an Indo-European language, distantly related to Latin and many European languages, including English.

Shakyamuni Buddha
Siddhartha Gautama, the historical Buddha. He was a prince of the Shakya clan in northern India who, many scholars now believe, lived in the late fifth and early fourth centuries B.C.E.

Soto
Zen school of Buddhism that traces its lineage to Hui-neng (638–713). It was revitalized and brought to Japan by Eihei Dogen.

Theravada

"The School of the Elders"; also the "Southern Tradition." One of the three main forms of Buddhism. Theravada is the form of Buddhism more prevalent in South and Southeast Asia: Sri Lanka, Thailand, Burma, Cambodia, and Laos. It remains a fairly cohesive whole, is more conservative in its attitudes and resembles most closely the Buddhism practiced during the Buddha's lifetime.

Tripitaka

"Three Baskets." The canon of Buddhist scriptures, consisting of three parts: the Vinaya-pitaka, the Sutra-pitaka, and the Abhidharma-pitaka. The first "basket" contains accounts of the origins of the Buddhist Sangha as well as the rules of discipline regulating the lives of monks and nuns. The second is composed of discourses said to have come from the mouth of Buddha or his immediate disciples. The third part is a compendium of Buddhist psychology and philosophy. The Tripitaka exists in distinct recensions, most notably Pali, Sanskrit, Chinese, Tibetan, and Mongolian, among others.

Vajrayana

"The Diamond Vehicle." One of the three main schools of Buddhism. By the eighth century, Vajrayana emerged in Central Asia: Tibet, Nepal, Bhutan, Mongolia, and eventually southern Siberia.

Vinaya

The Buddhist scriptures concerned with monastic discipline and moral conduct; rules for the behavior of the monks and nuns. One of the tripitaka of the Buddhist canon.

Zen

A major school of Chan Mahayana Buddhism, with several branches. One of its most popular techniques is meditation on koans, which leads to the generation of the Great Doubt.

Bibliography

Abbott, Elizabeth. *A History of Celibacy*. New York: Scribner, 1999.

Augustine, St. *Tractates on the Gospel of John 55–111*. The Fathers of the Church, vol. 90. Trans. John W. Rettig. Washington, DC: The Catholic University of America Press, 1994.

Augustinus, *Enarrationes in Psalmos 119–133*. Ed. Franco Gori. Corpus Scriptorum Ecclesiasticorum Latinorum, vol. XCV/3. Vienna: Verlag der Österreichischen Akademie der Wissenschaften, 2001.

The Book of the Discipline (Suttavighanga). Vol. I. Trans. I. B. Horner. London: Luzac & Company, 1970.

The Book of the Discipline (Vinaya-Pitaka). Vol. IV (*Mahavagga*). Trans. I. B. Horner. London: Luzac & Company, 1971.

Casey, Michael. *Strangers to the City*. Brewster, MA: Paraclete Press, 2005. Chapter 5, "Chastity."

Cassian on Chastity: Institute VI, Conference XII, Conference XXII. Introduction and Translation by Terrence Kardong. Richardton, ND: Assumption Abbey Press, 1993.

Dionysius the Pseudo-Areopagite: The Ecclesiastical Hierarchy. Trans. Thomas L. Campbell. University Press of America, 1981

The Dhammapada. Ed. K. Sri Dhammananda. Kuala Lampur, Malaysia: Sasana Abhiwurdhi Wardhana Society, 1988.

Dreuille, Mayeul de. *Seeking the Absolute Love: the Founders of Christian Monasticism*. New York: Crossroad, 1999.

Funk, Mary Margaret. *Thoughts Matter: The Practice of Spiritual Life*. New York: Continuum, 1998.

Griffin, John Howard. *Follow the Ecstasy: The Hermitage Years of Thomas Merton*. Ed. Robert Bonazzi. Maryknoll, NY: Orbis Books, 1993.

Grün, Anselm. *Celibacy—A Fullness of Life.* Trans. Gregory Roettger and Luise R. Pugh. Schuyler, NE: BMH Publications, 1993.

Kelty, Matthew. *Flute Solo. Reflection of a Trappist Hermit.* Kansas City, MO: Andres and McMeel, Inc., 1979.

———. *My Song Is of Mercy.* Ed. Michael Downey. New York: Sheed & Ward, 1994.

Merton, Thomas. *Cassian and the Fathers: Initiation into the Monastic Tradition.* Ed. Patrick F. O'Connell. Kalamazoo, MI: Cistercian Publications, 2005.

———. *Disputed Questions.* New York: Farrar, Strauss and Cudahy, 1960.

———. *Honorable Reader: Reflections on My Work.* Ed. Robert E. Daggy. New York: Crossroad, 1989.

———. *The Intimate Merton: His Life from His Journals.* Eds. Patrick Hart and Jonathan Montaldo. HarperSanFancisco, 1999.

———. *Learning to Love: Exploring Solitude and Freedom.* The Journals of Thomas Merton, vol. 6. Ed. Christine M. Bochen. HarperSanFrancisco, 1997.

———. "Notes on Love." *Frontier* 10 (Autumn 1967): 211–14.

———. *The Other Side of the Mountain: The End of the Journey.* The Journals of Thomas Merton, vol. 7. Ed. Patrick Hart, O.C.S.O. HarperSanFrancisco, 1998.

———. *The Springs of Contemplation.* A Retreat at the Abbey of Gethsemani. Ed. Jane Marie Richardson. First published by Farrar, Straus & Giroux, Inc., 1992. Notre Dame, IN: Ave Maria Press, 1997.

———. *Thoughts in Solitude.* New York: Farrar, Straus & Cudahy, 1958.

———. *Witness to Freedom. The Letters of Thomas Merton in Times of Crisis.* Selected and edited by William H. Shannon. New York: Farrar Straus Giroux, 1994.

Moore, Stephen D. *God's Beauty Parlor and Other Queer Spaces in and around the Bible.* Stanford, CA: Stanford University Press, 2001.

Murphy, Sheila. *A Delicate Dance: Sexuality, Celibacy, and Relationships among Catholic Clergy and Religious.* New York: Crossroad, 1992.

Nhat Hanh, Thich. *Freedom Wherever We Go. A Buddhist Monastic Code for the Twenty-first Century.* Berkeley: Parallax Press, 2004.

Pachomian Koinonia. Vol. II, *Pachomian Chronicles and Rules.* Trans. Armand Veilleux. Kalamazoo, MI: Cistercian Studies, 1981.

Panikkar, Raimundo. *Blessed Simplicity: The Monk as Universal Archetype.* New York: The Seabury Press, 1982.

Paulsell, William O. *Letters from a Hermit. With Letters from Matthew Kelty, O.C.S.O.* Springfield, IL: Templegate Publishers, 1978.

Pristas, Lauren. *The Theological Anthropology of John Cassian.* Ph.D. dissertation, Boston College, 1993. Ann Arbor, MI: UMI Dissertation Services.

The Rule of the Master. Trans. Luke Eberle. Kalamazoo, MI: Cistercian Publications, 1977.

The Rule of Saint Benedict. Trans. Leonard Doyle. Collegeville, MN: Liturgical Press, 2001.

Slater, Lauren. "Love, the Thing Called Love." *National Geographic* (February 2006): 32–49.

Stewart, Columba. *Cassian the Monk.* New York: Oxford University Press, 1998.

Participants in Monks in the West II
In order of seniority

Buddhists

Reverend Jisho Perry — Shasta Abbey, Mount Shasta, California (Soto Zen)

Reverend Heng Sure, PhD — Berkeley, Buddhist Monastery, Berkeley, California (Chan)

Venerable Jiru Bhikkhu — Mid-America Buddhist Association, Augusta, Missouri (Chan)

Lama Norbu — Bodhi Heart Center, Phoenix, Arizona (Tibetan)

Venerable Heng Lyu Bhikkhu — City of Ten Thousand Buddhas, Ukiah, California (Chan)

Reverend Heng Da [Thich Hang Dat] — Ten Thousand Buddhas Summit Monastery, Corydon, Indiana (Mahayana)

Ajahn Punnadhammo — Arrow River Hermitage, Thunder Bay, Ontario (Theravada)

Reverend Berthold Olson — Shasta Abbey, Mount Shasta, California (Soto Zen)

Bhante Dhammaratana

Bhavana Society
High View, West Virginia
  (Theravada)

Venerable Sudanto Bhikkhu

Abhayagiri Monastery
Redwood Valley, California
  (Thai Forest Tradition)

Reverend Kusala Bhikshu

International Buddhist
  Meditation Center
Los Angeles, California
  (Vietnamese Zen)

Venerable Jotipalo Bhikkhu

Abhayagiri Monastery
Redwood Valley, California
  (Thai Forest Tradition)

Catholics

Abbot John Klassen

Saint John's Abbey
Collegeville, Minnesota
  (Benedictine)

Father Terrence Kardong

Assumption Abbey
Richardton, North Dakota
  (Benedictine)

Father William Skudlarek

Saint John's Abbey
Collegeville, Minnesota
  (Benedictine)

Father J. P. Earls

Saint John's Abbey
Collegeville, Minnesota
  (Benedictine)

Father David Bock

New Melleray Abbey
Peosta, Iowa (Trappist)

Father Thomas Ryan

Paulist Office for Ecumenical
  and Interfaith Relations
New York, New York (Paulist)

Father Mark Serna

Portsmouth Abbey
Portsmouth, Rhode Island
  (Benedictine)

Brother Gregory Perron

Saint Procopius Abbey
Lisle, Illinois (Benedictine)

Father Ezekiel Lotz

Mount Angel Abbey
Mount Angel, Oregon
(Benedictine)

Father Michael Peterson

Blue Cloud Abbey
Marvin, South Dakota
(Benedictine)